T0354104

# Focus On Golf

## Creating The Golfer's Edge

By

## Edward A. Tischler

*AuthorHouse™*
*1663 Liberty Drive*
*Bloomington, IN 47403*
*www.authorhouse.com*
*Phone: 1-800-839-8640*

*First published by AuthorHouse    05/25/2011*

*ISBN: 978-1-4634-1487-0 (sc)*
*ISBN: 978-1-4634-1488-7 (dj)*
*ISBN: 978-1-4634-1489-4 (ebk)*

*Library of Congress Control Number: 2011908947*

*Printed in the United States of America*

# Table Of Contents

# Part Three:  Keeping The Process Fertile

# ACKNOWLEDGMENTS

*I'd like to give special thanks to the following people for their guidance, support, and friendship throughout the development of my game and teachings. Their contributions to the quality of my life have largely influenced my approach to the game and this book:*

My coach and mentor Fred Shoemaker whose guidance has helped open my life to what's truly possible and extraordinary. Along the way he has taught me how to be a real coach, while at the same time helping me achieve my true potential.

Michael Murphy and Timothy Gallwey for providing us all with *Golf In The Kingdom* and *The Inner Game Of Golf*. Their works have provided tremendous insights into the nature of the game we dream of playing. With the introduction of their approaches into my life, my game has always journeyed down a path that has been anything but traditional and ordinary.

My father, for setting a good example for me to follow. In doing so, he introduced me to the game while instilling in me patience, etiquette, sportsmanship, and a true love for the game.

My mother and the rest of my family for helping me forge through the trying times in my career.

All my students who continually re-commit to the journey. For they have taught me much about myself and coaching.

# New Beginnings

# Prelude

Since I was a boy I've been fascinated with the ability of accomplished performers to maintain their focus and composure in the most pressure filled situations. The feats of acrobats, martial artists, marksman, and all other precision athletes always intrigued me. Additionally, the best of the best in every sport seemed to make everyone else look simply average. I always wondered, what makes these performers so special? What type of edge did they have over everyone else?

As I played a variety of sports growing up, it became quite clear to me that having talent and ability was insufficient. Some of the most talented athletes have a tendency to fold under pressure, and some of the more averagely talented athletes seem to pull off the most magnificent plays when it most counts. In most sports even the best performers experience periods of slumps. However, there are those few that always seem to have an edge. They always seem to make the most of their abilities. With these observations in mind, my life became a quest for the answers to developing the edge.

Staying committed to this quest took me on an athletic journey. I played many sports in my youth, including gymnastics, tae kwon do, tennis, football, baseball, basketball, soccer, judo, water polo, archery, and of course golf. Since the first time I stepped on a driving range at the age of 9, golf was always my real passion. So when I turned 18 I made my first choice as an adult, I was to be a professional golfer. At that moment I committed my life entirely to golf, and golf became the venue for engaging in the quest.

Surprisingly the quest for the performance edge would lead me to the fields of philosophy, psychology, kinesiology, nutrition, fitness, awareness training, and personal growth. And through it all I've become a coach as well as a performer.

In 1992 I suffered a career threatening injury. I was unable to play golf for 4 years, incurred two surgeries, and underwent three years of physical therapy. In 1996 my doctors thought I'd never play golf again. However, I am happy to say I currently hold a +5 handicap. This seven-year journey to solve my physical problems provided me the opportunity to understand what truly makes the difference as a performer. Although my physical skills were neglected for many years, and although my body was much less fit than before my injuries, I was still able to score under par as soon as I was cleared to play golf. As a matter of fact, I shot 70 in my first round of golf after being cleared by my doctors to play. Since that round, I have regained my form and have become an even better performer, accumulating 8 hole-in-ones and setting over fifteen course records. So, what's made the difference, where did this performance edge come from?

Many of these answers came to me while coaching others to reach their potential. Though I was injured for all those years, I was still able to coach on a daily basis. As a coach I spent much of my time observing the habits, tendencies, mind-sets, and performance characteristics of my students. It was within those observations that many of the answers have been found. And most of them seem to be tied to the inner game.

As a player I had an incredible coach. He opened my eyes to what real coaching is all about. Early on he noticed my inquisitive nature, and he knew my thirst for knowledge would lead me to the arena of coaching. So, as my mentor he made the choice to share with me his insights into the field of coaching. Thus, I to became a coach. For that I am truly grateful, and I give thanks to my coach and friend Fred Shoemaker (author of *Extraordinary Golf*).

Coaches open doors, they inspire awareness, they observe patterns in behavior, and share their observations with their students. Coaches help students become aware of how their thoughts, beliefs, disposition, and response mechanisms affect their performance. Coaches help awaken their students to the processes of productivity, efficiency, cause and effect, habit formation, trust and confidence, and the way of being your genuine self. Coaches guide their students into enlightened states, where factors of performance become obvious and natural.

A coach's first step is to open the door to the way you'll eventually approach your life. Then the coach helps nurture that process. Your coach does so by helping awaken your senses, and that helps you become more in tune to what is going on in your environment. Awareness awakens you to true vision, effortless focus, unconditional confidence, and the freedom to be genuine in your actions. In short, coaches help you become aware of the state of being that guides you into the performance zone.

Volumes of instructional materials have been compiled with regard to the golfer's swing technique, and improvements in equipment and course conditions are well documented, however, the average golfers handicap has failed to improve over the past 40 years. Of course, instruction and technology do make the ball go further, which does influence the average golfers enjoyment and ego levels – if only briefly. However, that is insufficient for guaranteeing better performance, because once the golfers inconsistencies catch up to him, the enjoyment factor once again diminishes.

Let's take a peek into the state of being all accomplished players experience regularly. Accomplished players embody a sense of calmness and peace of mind. Their actions are free of tension and their focus is locked into target-oriented images. They are aware of their surroundings and committed to a game plan. Accomplished golfers are sure of the skills they possess, and understanding of the skills they are yet to internalize. With all this in mind, accomplished golfers maintain a productive disposition, one full of possibility and unconditional confidence. Finally, they appear to address the ball with calm preparation, they swing confidently, and they reflect on each performance with a sense of perspective.

The average golfer embodies a state of uncertainty. Their minds are full of mental chatter and they often entertain images of impending disaster. Average golfers are unsure of their skills and lacking in the necessary confidence. Therefore, the average golfer is full of anxiety, born of mental distractions, resulting in interference, followed by misdirected actions and emotional responses. Thus, average golfers address the ball in a state of tension, swing with either hesitation or aggressive fury, and react to their performances emotionally. Which way do you want to be on the golf course?

As you can see, there are considerable obstacles for the average golfer to overcome, whereas the accomplished golfer has learned how to by pass the obstacles by being focused and genuine in his actions. For the average golfer to become an accomplished golfer she, too, will need to develop a more confident and productive approach to golf.

Becoming an accomplished golfer involves changing the way you perceive the game. It involves developing a new way of being on the golf course. If you show up to the golf course with the same old habits, same old mind-set, and same old attitude, then it is unreasonable to believe that you'll have totally different and much more acceptable results. You must make a choice to change, and before you make the choice you must be willing to acknowledge that what you presently do fails to work in a satisfactory manner.

So, change is a process of awakening ourselves to the way we are, the way we act, the way we respond, and the way we continue from this point on. This means, we must be awakened to our way of being on the golf course. This begs the question, "Are your habits a hindrance or an asset on the golf course?" "Do you have a productive disposition, or do you act with hidden agendas lurking in the back of your mind?" Knowing the answers to these questions involves understanding your nature, and understanding your nature will involve the process of reflection. Are you willing to go there?

If you are unaware of your nature, then it will be difficult to depend on yourself in the moment of action. To understand your nature you'll need to observe your mental state and your response patterns. By observing your mental state as you prepare to play, you become aware of how your thoughts influence your choices and actions. And by observing your mental state as you respond to your actions, you'll become aware of how your thoughts influence your evolving attitude as well as your next move. This whole cycle involves a process of productive reflections, which is a developed skill.

There is an art to productive reflection. Reflections happen after the fact. They are observed and then we let go of them. If reflections become rumination, you become stuck in your mental conversations and detached from the moment. You become engrossed in habitual thoughts of past and future, and you get caught up in your expectations. As the habitual thinking is born, awareness is lost, the present recesses into the fog of internal conversation, the moment passes you by, and you are left being **MENTAL**.

It interests me that golf is commonly believed to be a mental game, I disagree. I feel that people are mental, and people become too mental during their play. Furthermore, being mental creates interferences that lead to distractions, and being distracted leads to misdirected actions. Remember, all inhibitions start with a mental process. Therefore, I feel it is beneficial for the golfer to be less mental. I feel each golfer would benefit from learning how to quiet the mind and open the senses. I believe the game is best played through the senses with an open mind and a genuine nature.

However, since people are mental, they need to be prepared for those moments when they become too mental, and they would do well to be committed to a process that will allow them to play more naturally, authentically, and without inhibitions. To do that, it is critical you understand your mental patterns and how they influence your productivity.

Being authentic involves being genuine in your behavior, being genuine in your responses to life's situations, and having genuine intentions at the beginning, in the middle, and in the end. Being genuine requires letting go of your social conditioning, freeing yourself from your habitual thinking, and clarifying your observations. Lastly, it involves making the choice to conduct yourself courageously, because being genuine can seem difficult once you've been conditioned to accept societal norms.

You may have noticed, it will take a lot of commitment to prepare yourself for that task. For preparation involves knowing your disposition and having the fortitude to honor your commitments. It means keeping your intentions clear and approaching your game with a sense of purpose, a purpose beyond the goal of simply scoring well. That purpose may involve acting genuinely while honoring your nature. And acting genuinely will involve being aware, fluid, in focus, and unconditionally confident. To achieve all that you'll have to let go of your mental tendencies and give into a natural state of being disposed.

So, with that in mind I'd like to know, "What is the next manifesting level of your game? Will your game become stagnant? Will you allow yourself to adapt and grow? Will you be stifled by your ruminating habits? Or, Will you manifest your being genuinely?" To do so, your preparation must provide a sound foundation, your actions must satisfy the basic needs of the game, and your responses will need to support your intentions.

In closing, to find your focal edge you'll need to create a new outlook about your game. This means, defining a path of productivity, establishing a disposition of unconditional confidence, awakening yourself to your true nature and honoring its authenticity. It means being true to yourself while understanding the nature of your mentality. This is the task of *Focus On Golf – Creating the Golfer's Edge*. I hope you enjoy the journey, and I invite you to join the quest.

"Being authentic involves being genuine in your behavior, being genuine in your responses to life's situations, and having genuine intentions at the beginning, in the middle, and in the end. Being genuine requires letting go of your social conditioning, freeing yourself from your habitual thinking, and clarifying your observations."

# Part One
## *The Golfer's Disposition*

# Chapter One
## *The Awakening*

If you want to change your game, it's time to awaken your mind and senses to a new way of approaching your golf. This awakening is about creating a new vision of how to play golf. It's about committing to a productive approach to golf. It's about considering how your beliefs, attitudes, and behavior habits influence your conduct on the golf course. It's about having a whole new outlook.

This outlook will consider the perspective of what's possible for your game instead of what's wrong with it. The average golfer is usually stifled by thoughts of what's wrong with their golf. I suggest you consider how to achieve what's possible? Every golfer knows their potential is much more than their present performance level. So, how about committing to work toward your potential?

Every time you step on the golf course, there exists the possibility that you will learn more about how to play your best golf. However, the only way you'll realize that is by being awake to the possibility when it happens.

If you fail to look for it, it will pass you by as it occurs. So, it helps to be looking for such possibilities. It helps to be looking in the right direction by having the perspective that it may occur.

Trying to fix what is wrong is a restrictive approach to golf. It's restrictive because it only considers what's out of place with regard to the skills you've already experienced. It neglects to consider the maximum potential of your game. If you were truly an awakened golfer, what skills would you possess?

Having that perspective will guide you down the path to your best golf. So, consider there's much more for your game than simply fixing your old incomplete game. Consider an ever growing and expanding game, one that will always offer you new levels of experience, enjoyment, and learning. And consider that such an approach to golf is right there in front of you. You simply need to see it that way.

The trouble is, your old beliefs and understandings create a smoke screen that covers your present perspective. The smoke screen hides the trailhead to your potential. If the trailhead is hidden, you will never find the path you desire. You might say your present beliefs camouflage the vision of what's possible. So, even when you are looking for it, it is hidden. Therefore, the awakening involves creating clarity with your vision. It's about awakening a crystal clear image of what's possible. As soon as you clear away the smoke screen, a new outlook will appear, an outlook expressing awakened views of life's potential.

# The Vision

The new outlook will contain a clear perspective. Having such a perspective is the foundation for growth and productivity. This is because, the type of perspective you create is the type of diet you feed your game. It is also because, your physical actions and behaviors follow the guidelines set down by your internal dialogues. All your inner workings, your beliefs, habitual thoughts, and ideologies create your present disposition. Your disposition is the underlying approach you have toward life. It defines your inclinations to act the way you do in each and every situation you face. Thus, it is a way of being created by and accepted by your inner self.

Your disposition, your attitude, your thought patterns, and your responses are all nurtured by your perspective. Therefore, you would be wise to create a perspective that is always concerned with providing the best nutrients to your mind, body, and spirit. In this way, perspective is the diet of being healthy and whole.

Such perspective is usually anchored in a code of understanding between willing participants. This code is more than a set of rules to be attached to. It is also different than a formula for success. It is more a vision, or an ideal, as to how awakened people conduct themselves. For example, soldiers abide by rules, regulations, and a chain of command; however, they live by a code of honor. The code of honor is simply a vision of how the ideal soldier conducts himself.

In ancient times, warriorship was the standard of conduct. The vision of warriorship was one of authenticity. A warrior was to strive to be genuine in every moment of life. A warrior would face every moment with the intent of being awake. She would approach each endeavor with unwavering commitment. A warrior never quits. Neither does a true golfer. Golfers have their own code of honor, their own ethics. We call it etiquette, and its founding principle is integrity.

Integrity is the ability to honor one's commitments. As my coach once put it, "The basis for his integrity is, you could say, his destinal resolve,..... a resolve that steers the course of his life. His goals, values and purpose in life have a foundation which I have rarely seen in my years of teaching. I can truly say that he is his own person and not simply the creation of various forces impacting on him in society. He has commitments in the various areas of his life, his relationships, his work and his golf, and not only are those commitments in alignment, but he honors them. That is what true integrity is."

The person who has integrity conducts herself with dignity. The warrior expresses dignity while honoring the code, and the golfer expresses dignity while honoring the game's etiquette. Honoring golf's code of etiquette means that you conduct yourself with dignity in all situations. Thus, to honor the code, you conduct yourself with dignity in all situations. Etiquette, integrity, and honor are always present to in the genuine golfer's disposition. This means dignity is the disposition of the honorable golfer.

The warrior's vision also included the principle that you always conduct yourself as if you were the role model for all those who will follow in your footsteps. You embody the principle so that those who look up to you for advice, guidance, and support will also understand the vision to follow. Thus, the vision expresses the time-tested ideal of leading by example. You can think about it this way, if everyone you ever touched wrote a note about how they remembered you, what type of conduct would you like them to associate with you – conduct yourself in that manner.

The last part of the vision is the idea that all warriors have a mutual respect for each other. Honoring the code with true integrity, and expressing their commitments with dignity, creates a type of bond between warriors. All warriors share a deep bond of mutual respect. The bond is so deep, it borders on friendship, even in the heat of battle. There are competitors in all sports that express that same virtue. However, it can be argued that the golfer that truly honors the etiquette of the game expresses it more than any other athlete.

Thus, golf truly is a game of honor. Real golfers honor the code and embody the vision while staying grounded in the game's self-policing rules and etiquette. Golfers are deeply rooted in the process of the game, a process that begins with their beliefs about how the game is meant to be played. The process is grounded by their understandings, nourished by their awareness, supported by their response systems, and sheltered by their commitments.

All warriors understand the process, they stay committed to the way, and find the source of their commitments within themselves, unconditionally as a universal truth. Furthermore, all warriors honor their commitments by their own volition. It is a choice to act in such a manner. It is a choice to conduct yourself with the vision in mind. It is a choice to honor your commitments. It is a choice to have fortitude. And so, for every golfer that wants to stay true to the path they too must make the choice.

# The Process

The warrior notices how her belief system and response mechanisms constantly influence the way she acts, learns, and perceives each moment of her life. Once again, all warriors understand the process, they stay committed to the code, and they find the source of their commitments unconditionally within themselves. So does the accomplished golfer. Understanding the way of the warrior is understanding the way of the competitor. Whether you compete in tournaments, or simply play recreational golf, you'll always be in competition with the course and yourself.

So, do your best to understand the way of the warrior-competitor. In the end, it will be the way of the golfer.

The way of the competitor begins with the code of honor. Next the competitor strives to understand what mode of play works best for himself. The competitor then creates a fluid game plan. A game plan which considers the chosen mode of play while allowing for adaptation and improvisation along the way. The ability to be fluid and adaptive is important, because the competitor knows that interferences can pop up at any point in the process.

The competitor knows that such interferences are just experiences as compared to something she owns. They are simply hiccups within her experiences. The competitor knows he has the skills to overcome and evade future interferences. The competitor knows that when you encounter interferences, you've simply ran into some bumps in the road. Your commitment ties you to the way and keeps you on track. If you honor your commitments then you honor the way, even if your journey is detoured from time to time.

Warriors and competitors respond well to the bumps and detours along the way. The way you respond is a sign of your true commitment. Do you respond with perspective? Do you react well to the mishaps on the golf course? Do you have a productive approach to assessing your play? The key is keeping perspective. And keeping perspective requires being awake and clear in your post-shot assessment process. Are you awake during your post-shot routine, or do you get stuck in self-absorbed analysis? Are you able to openly assess what just happened, or do you complain about your mishaps and bad fortune? Are you able to let go of your mishaps, or do you ruminate on your bad luck?

Whatever the case, if you are going to improve, you need to find a way to be more productive with the process. You might go as far as to say, you need to master the process.

# Mastering The Process

Mastering the way means being prepared to live life's challenges. It means having unconditional confidence in your ability to handle life's difficult moments. It means appreciating life's pleasurable times. It means having compassion for others when they struggle in life. It means being brave as you travel your own path. It means being genuine in your actions, which means being true to yourself and believing in your own validity.

Staying true to the course is difficult if emotions get in the way. Social conditioning often creates a belief system which has an emotionally sensitive foundation. That being the case, we may respond emotionally when the results of our actions are undesirable. Does that mean we are hot-headed or emotionally weak? Or does it simply means we have a tendency to react emotionally instead of with clarity?

Even with a strong disposition, emotions are a natural part of our response mechanism. Emotions are bound to kick-in at some point. The question is, what will you do next? How will you carry-on? Will you let go of the issue and get back into the game? Or will you dwell on the impetus for your emotional reaction?

When emotions habitually kick-in, strive to understand their nature. Dive into the habitual thoughts and beliefs that spark the emotional response. Clarify the fact that the emotions are interfering with your actions. Recommit to your potential and act genuinely by getting back into the game. So, be prepared to handle the struggles and be committed to getting back on track when you find yourself detoured. I always remind myself – **Get Back Into The Game.**

By this point you may have noticed reoccurring themes. These themes include the ability to prepare yourself properly, the ability to act genuinely, and the ability to react to your play with clarity and commitment to the vision. Keeping these themes in perspective, and laying a foundation that will continually support their presence is critical to the process of mastering your play.

Life is a continual journey, and the journey progresses in a cyclical manner. The game of golf also journeys in a cyclical manner, and your preparations, actions, and reactions define the basic cycle of your life and play. That being the case, mastering your play means being fluid with the transitions from preparation, to action, to reaction, to assessment, and to getting back into the game.

That may seem less exciting than learning how to drive the ball 300 yards. However, mastery is unconcerned with what's exciting. In fact, it is often more concerned with what's ordinary. My coach always told me, "Being extraordinary means performing ordinary tasks extra well, or extraordinarily well." And such is the path of mastery. Additionally, masters never tire of taking care of the fundamentals. Masters never tire of repetition. Masters never tire of their daily routines. Thus the accomplished golfer never tires of revisiting the fundamentals, of executing their routines, and of taking care of the game's cyclical process.

# Chapter Two
## *A Nurturing Attitude*

Chapter One may have seemed like an unlikely introduction on how to focus on golf. However, I believe the best place to begin any stage of learning is at the beginning. Growth in life always begins with the fundamental needs. These fundamental needs are nurtured by the conditions and nutrients presented by the current environment. Growth simply happens, and so does learning.

Now that you've created the fundamental vision by awakening your mind to a more productive way of being a golfer, you have given your game some life, you have given your game the basic life force needed for growth. It is now time to provide the proper conditions and nutrients so that improvement will simply happen. Simply put, you've planted new seeds by awakening a new vision of being a golfer. Let's make sure you keep those seeds planted in fertile soil, while at the same time feeding them the proper nutrients.

The process you engage in provides the conditions for growth. Your thoughts, beliefs, and reflections provide the nutrients. Therefore, maintaining a productive process will keep the conditions for growth fertile.

Additionally, understanding your thought patterns will help you understand the type of food you're feeding your game. Similarly, observing your beliefs and reflections will help you understand how well rounded your golf diet has become.

You can think of the process as the framework for conditioning. The process establishes the foundation for growth, and defines the parameters for action and observation. You might say the process guides you into action and helps you stay committed to the way throughout your responses. The process, therefore, is the soil you plant the seeds in. The nutrients on the other hand influence how you perceive life's happenings and that perception has a profound influence on the quality of your focus. More specifically, the thoughts, beliefs, and attitudes that create your underlying disposition are the nutrients that mold the way you perceive what's going on in your life.

Your perceptions affect your decision making process, your behavior patterns, and your performance levels. You would be wise to understand how your perceptions do that, and you would be wise to understand why your perceptions tend to reoccur in habitual patterns. We can find some of the answers by studying the nature of the mind and its conditioned thought patterns. So, once again it will help to consider what type of soil (the perspective and process) you've been planting the seeds in, and it will help to understand the type of nutrients (the thoughts, beliefs, and attitudes) you've been feeding your game.

Understanding your nature as well as your social conditioning will further clarify the reasons for your present conduct. This is because your nature will always influence your conduct authentically, while your social conditioning may impact your conduct in a biased manner. Your nature is founded in divine principles, and it always expresses itself genuinely. So, if your nature shines through and expresses itself in your actions, your actions will be natural and genuine.

If your social conditioning is nurtured through a process of being genuine, your conditioning will create a process of openness, clarity, and true perspective. Thus, the process you are engaged in will be truly productive. If your conditioning is malnourished by corrupted principles of social acceptance, your experiences will be filled with contradictions and conflicting views. That will cause hesitations and doubts to arise, and will inevitably render your journey less productive.

You can free yourself from your habitual patterns of behavior. You can change your conditioning. Remember, what you are conditioned to do is subjective, and it can be reconditioned. And, a productive reconditioning process can open your perception, awaken your senses, and clarify your observations. The result of such a reconditioning process is the restoration of your conduct to a natural way of being.

It may help to reflect on such concerns as, "How do I act when I express my true nature," and "What path to performance do my habitual thoughts guide me down?" Do your habitual thought patterns allow you to manifest your actions in a productive manner? Or, do they guide you into the non-productive process of rumination? Do your thought patterns facilitate the process of being task oriented, or do they lead you out of the present and into the fantasy worlds of expectations, what ifs, and woulda-shoulda-coulda's?

If your thought patterns continually lead you astray, then they are providing the wrong type of nutrients for your game – its hard to stay fit on a diet of ice cream and candy. If unhealthy thought patterns continually reoccur, I might suggest you ponder the question, "Where am I when my thoughts cease to exist?" I know for myself, when my thoughts become absent I find myself exactly where I am – aware of my present state of being. You might also inquire, "Who am I when my mind is quiet?" That one you'll have to answer for yourself.

Purity of action depends on having a present state of awareness. By being aware and fluid with your present focus, you are able to stay tuned into exactly what needs to be done. However, when thoughts are engaged and mental conversations begin, it becomes impossible to focus. Instead, you become stuck in the fantasy world of mental hypothesis. The what-ifs pop up, replacing the reality of what needs to happen, now. The woulda-shoulda-coulda's then support the story with Oscar winning performances. In the end, it was all an illusion. An illusion that turned into a nightmare, full of fear, doubt, frustration, and misdirected actions.

The only way around the fantasizing process is to make a commitment to being present more often. When you notice the nightmare thought process manifesting itself, make the commitment to snap out of the mental state and return to a productive process of awareness and absorption.

Getting back to a process of awareness and absorption can be facilitated by a mechanism for recommitment. You can use a saying as a trigger, you can use a mantra to restore your natural disposition, or you can use a meditative process to return to the present. There are many productive processes to choose from, you simply need to commit to one of them in the moment.

No matter what process you choose, choose one that keeps you grounded in principles that make the soil fertile. The main goal of that process will be to replace the non-productive patterns of thought and behavior with a healthy diet of awareness and genuine conduct. With that done you can get back to trusting your skills and playing enjoyable golf.

# Chapter Three
# *Being Genuine*

What does it mean to be genuine? Let's start with the question "How are you *being* while playing on the golf course?" What are your modes of preparation, performance, and purpose? What is your mode of responding, reframing, and recommitting to the cycle of golf? Do you have a clear process of preparation? Are you performance-oriented by clarifying and committing to the best courses of action? Do you find a way of being productive and purposeful in between golf shots? Do you respond well by assessing what happens and reframing your mind-set to stick to the chosen game plan? Do you follow-up your responses by recommitting to the process? Or is your play cluttered with being indecisive, hasty, and emotionally reactive?

Changing the way you play means changing *the way you are being* on the golf course. There are many things that define your being, and there are many things that influence *the way you are being* in the moment. Your actions, attitudes, and reactions are the obvious contributors to your mode of being a golfer. Your thoughts, beliefs, and underlying disposition provide some of the more subtle influences. However, the more subtle influences require your undivided attention. This is because the subtle influences are often harder to recognize. They also demand greater commitment to maintain productivity. Additionally, they have just as much impact as the obvious factors.

When a subtle influence sneaks up and catches you by surprise, it can often cause what I call a train-wreck. A train-wreck is the process of mental chatter turning into mental conversation, followed by distracted focus, resulting in poor performance, culminating in emotional reactions, and a loss of purpose. Then the cycle continues, snowballing and escalating into a state of being defensive and emotionally frustrated.

Most golfers have found themselves stuck in such a process. And I have yet to meet anyone that enjoys it. The whole process feels unnatural and unlike our true self. We all know it's non-productive, even unnatural, to act that way. We all know we'd *be* different if we were able to maintain our composure. We all instinctively know our best golf comes from within, from some place that houses our genuine nature. So, why do we get stuck in the process of habitual thoughts and train-wrecks?

We get stuck in the process because we are unaware of what causes us to act, or be, the way we are while playing on the golf course. Sometimes we fail to recognize the causes because they are extremely subtle. They are so subtle because they are the underlying fibers of our being human. So, if we are going to understand why we behave the way we do, we need to understand the underlying influences that cause us to behave the way we do.

Most golfers understand that their actions, attitudes, emotions, and reactions influence their performance and their score. However, they are unaware of how their upbringing, their social conditioning, and their belief system influences their play. I am often asked, "Why do I need to consider these factors, they have nothing to do with the rules and skills of golf?"

That may be so, however our actions are ultimately determined by our conduct. You have to play your way around the golf course with your skills, within the guidelines of the rules, while expressing your manner of being alive on this earth. When you are on the golf course, you are still existing as yourself, in your life. Escaping yourself, your humanity, your conditioning, and all the baggage you've accumulated in life simply because you are playing golf is impossible. Oh, sure you can try. And you may even succeed for brief moments at a time. But, your underlying disposition is going to catch up with you, especially during an activity that takes over 4 hours to play. So, the first parameter of life is, as long as you are alive you will find yourself in your life. Whether at work, home, or playing golf, you'd better find a way of being yourself that reflects a process of living well.

How do we live well? We do so by living our lives without carrying around all the unnecessary and negative baggage we humans tend to hang on to. It seems to me, the more baggage I carry with me the harder it is to act and react as my true self. It seems to me, the more baggage I carry around, the harder it is to be productive. It seems to me, the more baggage I carry around, the harder it is to reach my potential. Why, because negativity attracts negativity, and it has a tendency to drag us down.

For example, the more negative baggage I carry around, the less attractive my disposition appears to the people I meet. In some respects I become less presentable to the world. Other people sense the negativity and react to it. Other negative people may relate to it and be attracted to it, while more positive people will recognize it and want to stay away from it.

And, it is clear the more you surround yourself with negative people and negative influences, the harder it is to break out of the negative situation. Therefore, I choose to conduct myself in a manner in which I am more likely to attract productive people into my life. This will gravitate my life toward more productive situations and more productive opportunities, making it easier to reach my goals.

So, how do I live my life free of all the baggage? I can use meditation as a way of freeing myself from the bonds of negativity. I can use positive thinking to wade my way out of the swampland of negativity, or I can put blinders on in an effort to screen myself from potential negativity. However, even with such commitment it is likely that negativity will creep back into my mind.

Consider that there may be a way of being genuine right from the get go. There may be a way of being true to yourself that simply chooses to walk the other way when it sees negativity coming. There is a way of being that allows you to make the simple choices and commitments that will keep you living productively. And if there is, would that way of being provide you a better foundation for acting productively? Would that way of being keep your actions and responses true to the most genuine way of living? And, would that way of being shed light on your true potential? I think so!

Of course, using meditation, positive thinking, and blind faith as tools to guide you through tough moments can be helpful. However, I'd much rather stay committed to the process of being genuine in my life. What will your way of being genuine reveal about your true nature? Would you like to find out?

I associate being genuine with conducting yourself while honoring your divine nature. I believe we are all born into this world with a sense of living life as an expression of our true nature. I believe this is the purpose of life, and to its end I believe we are born into this life with a nature that is full of possibility. I believe our true nature is a divine gift, bestowed upon us for the purpose of reaching our potential.

I told my mom once, when I see old pictures of myself as a baby I had a certain look in my eyes. It reflected divinity, it had a genuine feel. That look stayed through my adolescent years, however, it slowly changed until enough of it was lost and what could be called "the look" was gone. I felt like I had lost that part of me. However, it could only be hiding because I knew it was inside me somewhere, deep inside. I told her, "I want that look back, it's mine, God's gift to me, and it shows me that I am perceiving life through my genuine nature."

When I peer into a baby's eyes I see the look. When I peer into a toddler's eyes I see the look 90% of the time. When I peer into a child's eyes I see the look 70% of the time. When I peer into a teen's eyes, I see the look 50% of the time. When I look into an adults eyes I see the look maybe 20% of the time. Why is it that we are born into this life with the sense of divine potential? Why is it that a baby's eyes look out into the world while reflecting this sense of potential? And why is it that an adult's eyes rarely reflect that sense?

I believe our eyes are the windows to our soul, and the soul is the gate-keeper of our genuine nature. Although we are born into this world with the purpose of reaching our potential through a process of acting genuine, social conditioning finds a way to introduce corrosive influences.

I also believe it is the job of the soul to guide us through life in such a way to maintain our original nature. However, the soul often becomes overly protective. It decides to shield our divine nature from the corruptive influences instead of mentoring us to deal with them in the most productive way.

If the soul decides to put up the shield to keep us from ever seeing these influences, the shield eventually becomes covered with corrosive influences. The more these negative influences pile up, the stronger the shield becomes. The tighter the gate-keeper locks up the doors you might say. Thus, the soul accepts the corruption in such a way to completely shield and isolate our divine nature from life's influences.

The more corrupt the process, the less the individual's genuine nature shines through. Thus, the look in the eyes changes. Even so, the individual's genuine nature keeps shining, it is simply hidden behind the corrosive coating the soul has accumulated. You might say, the sun is still shining behind the dark clouds of negativity.

In the film *Star Wars* they talk about the "Dark-Side" and the "Force." The dark side represents the over abundance of corruptive influences absorbed into the soul. The force represents the light of life, it expresses unconditional trust in one's divine nature. Even Darth Vader still housed the brightness of his genuine nature. He simply lost faith and chose to give into the influences of the dark-side. The lesson here is that the key to letting your divine nature shine through is to have unconditional trust in your genuine nature.

What the soul often forgets is one's genuine nature is incorruptable. It can be hidden, shielded, and locked away, but it can never become corrupted. Its essence is divine, its source is "the force." So, like an over protective parent the soul tries to shield, hide, and lock away the child from life's dark-side. However, in the end this over protective process fails, because it neglects to prepare the child for the inevitable meeting between life and its dark-side.

Good parents support and educate their children instead of committing themselves 100% to protecting their children. They also provide their children with the opportunity to learn from life, and to learn from their mistakes. They prepare their children for interaction in the world. They help their children learn the values of commitment, integrity, and honor. They impress upon their children the virtue of living, responding, and carrying on well in their lives. They show their children that having unconditional confidence in their true nature is the only validation they need as an individual. They show their children that trust is an indispensable tool in the process. They show their children by placing trust in their children. They trust that by nurturing the child's true nature, the child will consistently make good choices and learn from her mistakes.

Throughout this whole process the individual learns on her own the value of self. The individual learns to unconditionally commit to her true nature. And if the individual does so she will learn that her nature will always shine bright. In knowing this she will develop unconditional confidence in herself. For the only validation we need in life is knowing our own divine nature.

If we connect to our divine nature and commit to acting genuinely, we are being true to ourselves and we have nothing to be ashamed of. In the film *The Legend of Bagger Vance*, Bagger tells Junuh that he must find his authentic swing. He has Junuh watch Bobby Jones as he prepares to swing.

As they watch, they notice how Bobby Jones seems to be looking down the fairway in such a way to absorb himself and his swing into the field of play. At that moment, "the field" had very distinct energies connecting everything together, and Bobby Jones was simply trying to find his place in the field. For each moment, there exists an authentic swing for each individual. A swing that connects the golfer, the field of play, and the moment. And it is this swing, the one that is unique to us and the moment that is our authentic swing.

The only way you can act authentically is by believing in your true nature. At times that may seem hard to do. It involves unconditional commitment and faith. It involves letting go of your past and future. It means committing to the now through a sense of your own divine presence, "I am here to be myself and express my potential. It is my destiny, whether I realize it in this life or the next, and I will conduct myself while honoring its origins." This is the attitude of an authentic being.


The following quote from Ayn Rand's *The Fountainhead* also expresses this process. It is a tribute to the process of being genuine, of being true to oneself. The quote is from the introduction and I will pick it up here:

- "It is not the works, but the *beliefs* which is here decisive and determines the order of rank – to employ once more an old religious formula with a new and deeper meaning – it is some fundamental certainty which a noble soul has about itself, something which is not to be sought, is not to be found, and perhaps, also, is not to be lost.– *The noble soul has reverence for itself.–*" (Friedrich Nietzche, *Beyond Good and Evil.*)

This view of man has rarely been expressed in human history. Today it is virtually non-existent. Yet this is the view with which – in various degrees of longing, wistfulness, passion and agonized confusion – the best of mankind's youth start out in life. It is not even a view, for most of them, but a foggy, groping, undefined sense of raw pain and incommunicable happiness. It is a sense of enormous expectation, the sense that one's life is important, that great achievements are within one's capacity, and that great things lie ahead.

It is not in the nature of man – nor of any living entity – to start out by giving up, by spitting in one's own face and damning existence; that requires a process of corruption whose rapidity differs from man to man. Some give up at the first touch of pressure; some sell out; some run down by imperceptible degrees and lose their fire, never knowing when or how they lost it. Then all of these vanish in the vast swamp of their elders who tell them persistently that maturity consists of abandoning one's mind; security, of abandoning one's values;

practicality, of losing self-esteem. Yet a few hold on and move on, knowing that the fire is not to be betrayed, learning how to give it shape, purpose and reality. But whatever their future, at the dawn of their lives, men seek a noble vision of man's nature and of life's potential.

.....It does not matter that only a few of each generation will grasp and achieve the full reality of man's proper stature – and that the rest will betray it. It is those few that move the world and give life its meaning – and it is those few that I have always sought to address. The rest are no concern of mine; it is not me or *The Fountainhead* that they will betray: it is their own souls. *Ayn Rand   New York, May 1968"*

That passage has captivated me since I first read it, and its essence has stayed with me my whole life. I, too, believe that, "*The noble soul has reverence for itself."* I believe such a soul honors life's commitments with true integrity, and I believe such a soul acts with dignity, with the intention of being genuine in one's conduct.

If we are born into this life with such a genuine presence; If we are born into this life with such divine purpose; then we ought to honor that intention by feeding purposeful fuel to the fire, instead of dishonoring it by trying to smother it out through corrosive philosophies and corruptive social acceptance. So, since we are born into such a noble presence, let's seek a way of living that expresses its genuine being? Let's commit to living life in a most genuine manner?

Of course, even that idea is a philosophy, a sort of ideology about a better way of life and play. You'll have to decide for yourself whether being genuine in your actions is a better way of being on this earth, in this lifetime. You'll have to decide for yourself whether being genuine in your conduct will help you realize your potential. You'll have to decide for yourself whether being genuine in your responsive behavior will help keep you true to the path of better play.

I do know this, if you never give being genuine a try, then you'll never know how it can influence the quality of your life and play. Conversely, if you commit to being genuine in your conduct, your actions, and your behavioral responses, you will certainly know how it influences the quality of your life. And remember, when you are playing golf, your life is golf for the moment. So, I urge you to seek your genuine nature, to become best friends with your original self, and to commit to being as authentic as possible until you understand its influences.

# Chapter Four
## *Being Open-Minded*

As we got started on this journey, we awakened a new vision of how life and golf can be. Next we discussed the type of disposition needed to establish a nurturing attitude. Continuing the journey led us to recognizing our genuine nature. Now it is time to institute the last piece of the fundamental process, Being Open-Minded.

Being open-minded means putting aside the pretense that we know all we need to know. It means being wise enough to know, the only way we can continue to grow is to be open to new information and new ways of looking at life.

I often hear people say, "Yeah, I'm open to new suggestions." Then I wonder, how open are they really. Are they willing to put aside all their beliefs, all their experiences, and all their conclusions about life to give a new approach a chance? I wonder, are these people open to the idea of reinventing themselves on the spot if need be? This, to me, would be truly open minded – willing to put aside all that you think you know so that you can completely absorb yourself into a new aspect of life.

As we go through life, experiencing new events, new ideas, and new situations, we create an understanding about how things work and what works best for us. The more often we experience like situations, we accept the idea that we know, before the fact, how things work. At that moment we have created a preconception. The next time we think we are encountering a similar situation, we have already preconceived ideas in mind.

These preconceptions create a filtering process. By using the information we already know to categorize and associate incoming information with past information, we are filtering the incoming information to see where it fits in our understanding. Sometimes, these filters become so strong that they actually prejudice the incoming information. The filter may prejudice the information simply because of the source it is coming from. If you believe so strongly that a certain type of person is bad, then you may be unwilling to listen to anything that person has to say, even if he has something perfectly correct to express. That is being prejudiced.

Now, if you are suspicious of a source's validity, for whatever reason, but you allow the information in, compare and associate it with your knowledge base, study it further through new and open research, you are filtering the situation productively. You are putting your prejudice aside.

A true prejudice leaves little room for a change in view, a filter allows for the change, however it usually does so while mixing in some of the old with some of the new. This gives it a twist. The result is a clouded version of the new information. Clouded because it is slightly tainted by the filtering process, even if the new information gets through. A truly open mind is without prejudice. It entertains new information, even in the presence of preconceptions. It would receive the new information absolutely before it began to compare it with the already existing knowledge base.

When I was a boy taking Tae Kwon Do lessons, I was introduced to a story told by Bruce Lee. The story was called Empty Your Cup. I later found out that it is a famous tale used widely in eastern philosophy. The story told of a student that was so eager to learn and apply what was being taught that his mind was too full of ideas. This student asks his master a question regarding how long it would take to master the necessary skills. At that moment, the master started to pour the student a cup of tea. As the tea filled the cup to the brim the master kept pouring the tea and the tea overflowed onto the table. The student yelled, "Master, stop, the tea is overflowing." Then the master told the student, "Your mind is like this cup, if you keep it too full of ideas, there will be no room for new information, in which case it will take you several life times to master the skills. If you want to learn the skills in a timely manner, you will first need to empty your mind's cup before every lesson. You will need to prepare your mind by opening it to whatever the lesson has to offer without injecting your ideas into the moment."

This story has been told many times in a variety of different ways, but the moral of the story is always the same. The more full you regard your accumulation of knowledge and skill, the less room there is to accumulate more knowledge and skill. So, learn to empty your cup of knowledge when you step into the learning environment.

When a person empties her cup she is often said to be returning to the beginners state of mind. A true beginner feels void of the information needed to be accomplished in any walk of life. A true beginner is eager to seek out, research, and put into action any thing that will fill the void purposefully. A true master knows that there is always an infinite amount of learning to be experienced.

Therefore, a true master is always ready to empty her cup and return to the beginner's state of mind. Without such an open mind-set, the master knows she will be uncoachable.

Students often come to lessons with hidden agendas lurking in their minds. They often hide their true concerns, unable to air them out with the coach. Therefore, the students fail to state their true purpose for taking the lesson, and in turn fail to empty their cups. These students are often too full of their own ideas, issues, and beliefs. They are so preoccupied with the possibility of the coach leading them down an undesirable path that they never state what they really want. These students have trouble explaining their reason for coming to a lesson without qualifying every point, and they often have trouble listening. Therefore, they filter all the coach has to say, while trying to avoid the possibility of the coach guiding them astray.

These students often express an urge to impress the coach with the fullness of their knowledge. They seem to feel the need to take control of the learning process. In which case they try to tell the coach how to coach. "I'm best coached this way," or "I'm this type of learner" a coach will often hear. Does that mean they have exhausted all other alternatives, or are these simply the alternatives the student has already found functional?

In the end, these students become unwilling to be guided to the answers. They've put up so many barricades and detours with their neglect to be up front with their coach that it is almost impossible for the coach to awaken new points of awareness. Even if the coach finds a way to help the student entertain a new point of view, there is rarely enough room to accept the concept into the mind's cup.

Filling your mind with knowledge to combat new points of view is being closed-minded. Harboring hidden agendas as you venture into new experiences is being closed-minded. And feeling the need to control the learning environment is being closed-minded.

Be open to receive and experience what your coach has to offer. Listen to what is being said, and try to understand what is being communicated. Make a commitment to return to the beginners mind, then allow your experiences to prove the lessons validity.

Putting an open-minded approach into practice is achieved by committing to it on a daily basis. For me, every morning I awaken to an empty cup, eager to fill it with new understandings. At the end of the day's events I put it all in perspective. Then as I fall asleep I let it all go into every cell of my being where it can find its place with perspective. Once again, I will awaken open-minded, ready to learn freely.

Freedom is the ability to let go of oneself completely, only to be reborn to a new perspective in the next moment. Every moment of life gives you the opportunity to recreate yourself before emptying the cup once again. Freedom also means freeing yourself of expectation as well as your past.

An open mind is free to experience and accept what comes next. An open mind is free to consider every opportunity that comes its way. An open mind operates without considerations of what to expect. Thus, an open mind is truly a free mind.

Productive students are willing to unveil what is being communicated by the coach. They are also open to the prospect that the coach merely presents the guidelines to a productive approach to learning. The productive student considers that he may need to fill in the gaps and extend the process on his own, especially in between meetings with his coach.

Productive students understand that too much filtering without open-minded understanding muddies the waters of learning. Productive students know that closed-minded filters create waves in the learning process. And the stronger the blinders, the bigger the waves. So, productive students do their best to keep the process of learning fluid and enlightening.

Do you have rigid, expecting agendas as you go thru the day, or do you approach life with an open willingness to learn? Do you look for specific answers only to miss the ones being presented in the moment? Do you think you know what type of answers will work best for you, or are you open to a new perspective?

If you are going to improve, you need to learn something new. If you need to learn something new, you need to realize there is more to be learned. And that will require you to adjust your perspective, or even create a whole new perspective. Entertaining a whole new perspective offers you more opportunity to find the adjustments. You can look at it this way, if what you are doing fails to work, reframe it. Close your eyes, take some deep breaths, and create a perspective that works. Or, if nothing else, simply clean the mental slate so that you can begin to look at life openly. Once again, to do this you must be willing to let go of all you think you know.

Being truly open minded also means having the ability to look at life outside the conditioned framework of social norms. It means finding a way to step out of the situation and see the whole situation for what it is. Being open-minded means considering all possibilities and all options, even if they are unconventional.

Furthermore, being open-minded means being willing to try new drills, new exercises, new swing styles, and new coaching techniques. It means you are willing to follow the guidance of your coach even if you only partially understand why you are being guided down the present path. Sometimes it takes continued training before the experiences come alive.

I know for myself, my coach often gave me drills and exercises that only revealed their true importance after I performed them consistently for many months. They always had some basic purpose, however, the magic of the exercise was only revealed to the dedicated practitioner. Therefore, to be truly open-minded, you must be openly willing to return to the roots and the basic exercises over and over, until their hidden secrets are revealed to you.

Finally, being truly open-minded means being open to alternative courses of action, such as laying up on a reachable, yet extremely guarded approach shot. Such as, playing for bogey from time to time. Such as, playing into a greenside bunker on purpose. Such as, playing an approach shot long left when the pin is guarded back right. Such as playing a shot to the middle of the green when the pin is tucked over a bunker.

There are many situations on the course that favor aiming for the rough or away from the pin. There are even more occasions when playing to miss a green on purpose is more appropriate then going for the pin. These concepts seem foreign to the mind-set publicized in today's golf community. Fairways and greens, fairways and greens, is constantly preached. And that may be recommended as the basic game plan, however, I encourage you to also keep your options open. For example, sometimes I plan to drive the ball into a greenside bunker on a short par four. Sometimes I find it appropriate to aim for the rough so that I have a better angle to a tucked pin on my approach shot. And if I find myself out of position, I might lay up if I am confident I can get it up and down for par.

So, being open-minded means being willing to approach each moment of life without a filtering mentality. It means being willing to follow your coach's guidance. It means establishing a productive mind-set, and freeing your mind to be reborn everyday and in every situation you encounter. It means being willing to set your normal thought patterns aside and starting to look at your situation as an outside observer. Lastly, it means keeping your options open while being open to alternative courses of action.

# Part Two
## *Cornerstones for Improvement*

# Chapter Five
## *Readiness: The Goal of Preparation*

The goal of preparation is to ready yourself for the task you intend to fulfill. To be truly ready, you must commit 100% to the course of action you'll take. And that requires that you only choose skills that are ready for use. You must be 100% certain of your ability to perform the skills, and you must be willing to express fortitude, your ability to forge on through pressure filled times. Therefore, to be truly ready, understand the process in its entirety, and clarify the process in such a way to give your actions purpose.

We've often heard great players, such as Jack Nicklaus say "The set-up is 90% of the battle." To the same end, we hear that preparation is 90% of the battle. The reason for this view is that your preparation lays the foundation for your future. The quality of your preparation will ultimately determine whether you were ready to handle the events that followed.

Being truly prepared means having everything in perspective. If your perspective is so clear that your course of action is unquestionable, you can simply do it. With all mental concerns in their place, you simply perform the physical action. Therefore, being truly prepared means that you are so ready to do it that you can act without hesitation, without mental interference. For these reasons, I believe playing golf is mostly mental for golfers that lack preparation, and mostly physical for golfers that are truly prepared.

Your preparation has more to it than simply performing some set-up procedure. Your preparation has more to it than performing a pre-shot routine. Your preparation involves your ongoing education. Your preparation involves your evolving attitude. Your preparation involves the expansion of your mind-set. Your preparation involves the strength of your imagination. Your preparation involves the quality of your fitness. Your preparation involves your understanding of course design and course management. Your preparation involves the internalization and maintenance of your skills, and your preparation involves the cultivation of your focus.

So, the more prepared you are the less likely you'll become too mental during your play. Being mental is simply entertaining mental distractions, thoughts that distract you away from the task of performing the physical actions. There are interferences that can be considered physical. Such as a startling sound, a physical injury, or blinding glare produced by a setting sun. However, even these distractions can be overcome through extreme absorption into the process. As a matter of fact, whether loss of focus is caused by daydreaming, blackouts, lack of confidence, mental chatter, or a physical stimuli, all interferences can be overcome through preparation and total absorption into the physical actions of the game.

As you can see, preparation is a time consuming process. You train, you study, you refine, you re-educate, you internalize, you assess, you create plans, execute, re-assess, and recommit. You choose a purpose and honor it with your actions, your reactions, and your ongoing choices. And you voluntarily engage in this ongoing process so that at some moment in the future you are ready to perform a task that will only last 2 seconds.

Each and every time you stay 100% committed to the process you solidify your preparation for the next time you need to perform the task. Additionally, what you do in between performances becomes the newest addition to your ongoing efforts to become prepared. Furthermore, the process becomes more involved when you consider that you must be prepared to handle all the putting, chipping, pitching, sand, approach, and driving situations that show up on the golf course. The more prepared you are to handle the present situation, the more readily you'll perform the necessary skills. Therefore, preparation is the price you pay for being ready to handle life's challenges. Think of the commitments an Olympic athlete makes. They spend a minimum of four years studying, training, and developing focus and confidence. They commit to fitness, nutrition, and strict routines. In short, they dedicate every moment of their waking hours for four years to reach a critical moment. Then in a blink of an eye the moment is done. Four years of preparation comes down to one moment, and the quality of those four years of preparation reflects on how well they faced the final situation. Were they truly ready, did they do their best, bronze, silver, or gold medal aside.

In life and in golf your preparation is never done, it's an ongoing process. It's the foundation of your readiness, and it's at the core of your productivity. So, you would be wise to learn all you can about what it is to be truly prepared. Once you've done so, I'm sure you'll find your performances routinely extraordinary. You simply need to find the desire and commitment to never tire of the preparation process.

Beyond maintaining the commitment to preparation, you may need some guidelines as to the structure of being ready. For example, you will need to develop and maintain the fundamental skills of golf. These skills include the obvious physical techniques of putting, chipping, pitching, iron play, playing the woods, and any other specialty shots. And you can develop these skills with the help of a suitable coach. Beyond these physical skills, you can seek the help of an athletic trainer or postural conditioning coach to develop and maintain the needed fitness level. This will certainly round out your physical preparation. Of course, this book is more concerned with developing your inner skills, because they are what influence the golfer's edge the greatest. So, we will leave the physical game aside for now.

The mental side of your game will also need to be considered in the preparation process. You'll need to educate yourself with regard to course design, management, shot strategies. You'll need to become more aware of how your thinking patterns influence your attitude, your choices, your beliefs, commitments, and disposition. And, you'll need to understand the nature of the mechanical mind and how it has a tendency to create mental interferences that disrupt the process of focus. Lastly, you'll need to understand how to quiet, or pacify, the mind so that your skills can be applied naturally and efficiently.

Preparing your inner game for the task of playing golf will involve opening your senses. It will involve developing your skills of awareness. It will involve heightening your levels of confidence, both subjectively and unconditionally. Readying your inner game will involve establishing a productive disposition, solidifying your commitments, monitoring your behavior habits, and strengthening your integrity, your honor, your fortitude, and your sense of warriorship.

With all this in mind, preparing your physical, mental, and inner qualities will involve all aspects of your life. It will encompass the way you approach and respond to every moment of your life. It will involve your actions, reactions, and your ability to "stay the course."

Being a willing participant in the ongoing process of preparation is the cornerstone to readiness, the primary footing for success, and helps establish the confidence needed to possess the golfer's edge. If you are unwilling to make the preparation commitment, then it is unlikely you will reach your goals. Preparation demands total commitment to the "Way." It's a way of life, and for golf it is the "Way of the Golfer." Without such commitment you will never develop the Edge. Are you going to be ready when the time comes, will you prepare yourself adequately?

Let's get you started on the preparation process by establishing guidelines, as well as exercises, that can regularly help you heighten your level of preparation. The guidelines will be in the form of the commitments you will make on a daily basis. I'll list some commitments to get you started. You can use the one's I provide, or you can review them and write down some of your own. Even if you choose ones I have provided, I want you to write them down on your own piece of paper. I want you to post the list somewhere in your home, office, and/or car. Post it in a place where you are certain to see it every day. When you see the list, I want you to read it carefully, absorbing your attention into the importance of commitment.

~ 50 ~

If you truly want to solidify each commitment, read the list out loud. Vocal affirmation is one of the strongest tools we have for maintaining our commitment and self-motivation. You may feel funny saying it out loud at first. However, you'll get used to it, and you'll come to value the powers that work through vocal affirmation.

The following pages will show that much of the preparation process is fulfilled through upholding your commitments and paying attention to your behavior patterns. The rest of the process involves believing in the vision of how you want to be and play on the golf course, studying course design and course management techniques, knowing your disposition, discovering the nature of your mind and your habitual patterns of thought, and developing the powers of your mind's eye.

Clearing the daily interference out of your mind helps you become better prepared for practice and play. You may notice that the exercises help you learn how to keep score of your commitment levels. For example, by rating how focused you are, by rating how much conviction you maintain, or by noticing how confident you are, you gain a more clear understanding of what works and what fails. Get to know this preparation process, and commit to being as prepared as possible by considering all aspects that influence how ready you are for playing the game.

# Commitments To Solidify The Preparation Process:

- I will prepare my attitude by making a commitment to only comment on the positive aspects of my play. If it is difficult to find something positive to say about my play, then I will find something positive to affirm about life.
- I will prepare my response mechanism by imagining how I will react to misplayed shots on the course. I will imagine conducting myself as an honorable golfer.
- I am committed to having fortitude by believing in the value of forging through the trying times with a sense of humor and humility. I will commit to smiling in the face of adversity.
- I am committed to accepting only productive thoughts into my mind, and I will commit to letting the unwanted visitor thoughts leave my mind as quickly as they snuck in.
- I am committed to learning more about how golf courses are designed, and how I can manage my way around the course with a more prepared game plan.
- I am committed to becoming more aware of my underlying disposition, and I am committed to becoming more aware of the type of disposition I have when I play my best golf.
- I am committed to understanding the reoccurring conversations that pop into my mind and interfere with my focus.
- I am committed to use only the skills I am confident in when I am on the golf course.

Write down, on a separate piece of paper 3 to 4 commitments of your own. You can choose from the examples above, or choose ones more suited to your golfing needs. Choose commitments that will make a real difference in your game, then find the conviction to back up your commitments.

## Exercises To Solidify The Preparation Process:

- I will rehearse my set-up and my posture in front of a mirror so that I can address my shots with poise and balance.
- I will swing with my eyes closed every day to awaken my senses to the feelings of my swing.
- I will practice exhaling as I swing to learn more about how I can swing in a truly relaxed manner.
- I will prepare my course management skills by playing the course in my mind's eye before I fall asleep the night before I play the course.
- I will keep score of how many shots I play in each round that had total conviction backing them up, and I will calculate what percentage of the total shots played had such conviction.
- I will keep score of how often bad attitudes and negative thoughts invade my game by making an X on the scorecard each time it happens. And I will notice whether I play better with more or less X's on my card.
- I will exercise regularly, for strength, flexibility, endurance, and good posture.

- I will empty my mind's cup before each lesson. I will take a few minutes to remind myself that I am here to learn something new. I am here to be coached into some new understanding the coach has to offer. I freely choose to follow my coach's guidance.
- I will take a few moments to close my eyes, feel my breath, and restore my natural rhythm before I get out of my car and head for the pro shop. This will put the events of the day aside so I can clarify why I am at the golf course.

Write down 2 to 3 exercises that will help you become more prepared. Then commit to practicing these exercises as regularly as possible.

# Preparation Considerations:

The following list can help you understand what you are most prepared to do, and what preparation considerations need more attention. Check this list from time to time and rate on a scale from 1 to 10 (1 for barely prepared, and 10 for 100% prepared) how prepared each aspect is at the moment. The more often you check the list and rate each consideration the more clear it will be why you play the way you do. Eventually, you'll find the self-motivation to get all aspects as prepared as possible. Make some photo copies of the list so you have extras ready to use periodically.

## Periodically check this list and assess how prepared you really are:

### Physical Considerations                              Rating
### From 1 to 10
Putts (Short, Mid, Long)
Short Game (chip, pitch, lob)
Wedge Play
Irons (Short, Mid, Long)
Utility Clubs
Fairway Woods
Driving
Sand Shots
Physical Fitness
Posture

### Mental Considerations                               Rating
### From 1 to 10
Positive Mind-Set
Remembering The Fundamentals
Remembering The Process
Game Plan Selection
Clarifying Your Choices
Making Decisive Choices
Noticing Visiting Thoughts as they Pop-Up
Letting Go of Unwanted Thoughts
Quieting The Mind
Visualizing Your Shots
Subjective Confidence

## Inner Game Considerations                    *Rating*
## From 1 to 10
Eyes Closed Awareness
Relaxed Breathing
Imagining the Chosen Swing
Absorption and Trust in the Process
Unconditional Confidence
Commitment to Your Choices
Knowing Your Disposition
Fortitude to Forge on without Negativity
Resolve to Always Recommit to the Game Plan
Being Purposeful
Maintaining Composure

# Chapter Six
## *Performance: The Goal of Action*

The goal of action is performance. The higher the level of performance you desire, the more focused your actions need to be. High levels of focus require confidence in your physical skills, clarity in your imagination, and trust in your powers of absorption. All actions are process-oriented. The action itself is unconcerned with the result, it is only concerned with being the action that is the process. If you are action-oriented then you are process-oriented. So, good performers learn how to commit to the actions without interfering thoughts taking hold of their minds.

When high levels of performance are desired, you can only commit to the actions you know you are ready to perform. There is zero room for experimenting when performance is the goal. Remember, experimenting is a process of seeking out and developing new actions. Performance is about applying the actions you've already internalized. There is zero room for indecision when performance is your goal. There is zero room for wandering thoughts, scattered attention, or disoriented focus when performance is your goal. Performance requires total absorption into the chosen actions.

Your performance routine will use three basic steps to guide you into the actions: (1) Make sure you choose actions that are ready to be confidently used, (2) Choose a game plan that utilizes your strengths, and (3) Absorb yourself totally into your shot routine until you feel fully ready to pull the trigger.

If you stay committed to all three steps, the actions will simply be a reaction to the process, and your level of performance will match your level of conviction. It takes a lot of preparation to be truly ready to execute this performance routine, and it takes a lot of conviction to stay the course. Remember, half-hearted conviction will lead to failure, which means all your preparatory efforts have gone to waste. Make a commitment to choose the actions that are ready to be used, make a commitment to choose a game plan you can believe in, and make a commitment to absorb all your attention into the process.

Remember, absorption is a matter of becoming the role, just like an actor does. Believe you are the type of golfer you have been training to be. Put all your imagination, all your feelings, emotions, intensity, and resolve into being the type of golfer you want to be. Only approach the ball when you've found total commitment. Only pull the trigger once you are totally committed to the choice you have made for the situation that is presented right in front of you, at this moment. If there is any doubt as to the available skills, the chosen game plan, or the application of resolve, then your performance level will suffer. This is unacceptable if performance is the goal.

A true performance-oriented golfer concerns herself with the process of executing an effective performance routine (shot routine). What makes the process effective is making sure that you make the right choices and back them up with conviction and total absorption. I know, "How many times is he going to mention the three steps of the performance routine that guide us into action?" Even though I am hesitant to make this chapter seem too repetitive, the fact is, I believe it is *imperative* that these three steps be burned into your memory banks.

Whenever you think about playing golf, I want you to remember the process. Whenever you step on the golf course I want you to assess your preparation level, choose a course of action you can believe in, and absorb yourself totally into the process. Each time it is your turn to play I want you to apply these steps whole-heartedly. If you stay committed to this process, I guarantee you'll enjoy a higher level of performance. Once again, it is impossible to overemphasize these three steps; they are the cornerstones of performance.

So what types of choices are you going to make when performance is on the line? What type of actions are you going to use when it's time to get the job done? Will you choose actions you are confident in? Will you create a game plan you can believe in? Will you truly absorb yourself into the process?

Great performers know their skills, their strengths, and their limitations. Great performers know there are more important things than being the strongest, the most talented, or the most gifted person. Great performers know they must be the most prepared. Great performers know they must be the most committed to the process. Great performers know they must have clarity in their vision, clarity in their actions, and clarity when absorbing themselves into the chosen course of action.

It is a process. Preparation followed by vision, choice, absorption, and reaction. Your preparation and your performance routine bring you to the critical moment of action. As your performance routine moves you into the moment, you give into it completely. If you fail to do so, you are certain to entertain mental thoughts that will create uncertainty. If you absorb yourself completely into the process whole-heartedly, you will simply react when the moment comes. If you entertain mental thoughts, you will experience doubts and hesitate instantaneously before reacting to your doubts. What would you rather do, react to a process of clarity and absorption, or react to a process of doubt and hesitation? If you are having trouble figuring it out, reacting to clarity and absorption will bring about the desired performances, while reacting to doubts and hesitations will bring about what you fear. Once again, your level of conviction with regard to the process will determine how well you perform. So, achieving the desired level of performance simply becomes a matter of committing to the process.

Everyone can be committed enough to perform well, they simply need to believe in the process. Everyone who believes in the process and keeps their attention on the actions will always be performance-oriented. Instead of being performance-oriented, many golfers become perfectionists. They seek out the imperfections in their actions and try to eliminate them. They become more concerned with preventing errors than they are with performing the ready to use skills. They become so concerned with their mistakes that they often forget the basic need to get the job done.

Other golfers avoid performance by constantly tinkering with their game. It's as if they believe there is one magic move that is free of limitations. That's like searching for a pot of gold under a rainbow. Those golfers find more value in experimenting than they do in performing. Although effective in the learning process, both tinkering too much and striving to be a perfectionist will eventually cause problems in performance. So, learn to leave the tinkering for the practice area, learn to look at what's working now, and focus on the process of performance when you are on the golf course.

Some golfers have all the tools to play the game well, but lack the conviction to play within the performance mode. If that is your case, you would be wise to isolate the process and clarify how you will stay the course of being process oriented. To stay the course of performance you need to know the process inside and out. The process needs to be clarified and organized. So let's get organized. Get a piece of paper and divide it into three columns. In those three columns we are going to clarify what you need to do to solidify the process. If you routinely perform this exercise, you will easily identify what areas of your game are ready to be used in play, which ones need more preparation, and which ones simply need more conviction in the application process.

Divide the paper into three columns. At the top of the first column write the heading, "Physical Skills." At the top of the middle column write the heading, "Game Plan." At the top of the third column write the heading "Inner Conviction."

Before you use the evaluation chart I want you to choose two holes you play regularly. Choose one hole you play well and one hole you play poorly. Now, review the way you play each hole. Notice whether you have a decisive game plan and whether you feel confident or doubtful. When reviewing the way you play these holes, notice that the hole you play well tends to fit your strengths. You probably feel confident in your shot selections and your game plan, and you probably stay committed to the plan. You probably do a good job of imagining how you want to play each shot and simply react to your images. Additionally, these holes are played without intervening thoughts, without doubts popping up, and without hesitation.

When reviewing the holes you play poorly, notice that the design may challenge your weaknesses, or maybe it fails to fit your eye. Something about the hole may simply look funny to you. Maybe you believe, "I should be able to make birdie even though it continues to get the best of me." Whatever the case, you continue to make choices that fail to work. In that situation, you second-guess your choices, you habitually create doubts about what you should do, and you hesitate before you act, bringing unwanted actions into existence.

Do you recognize a difference in your disposition on each of those holes? Do you realize that you are being two different types of golfers, on two different holes, on the same golf course, within one round of golf? Let's break that pattern. Let's learn how to choose and execute a more performance-oriented routine. To do that you may need to give up your own personal par on your nemesis hole. Instead of planning for par, plan for bogey. Golfers planning for bogey make a lot of bogeys, a few pars, and very few others. However, golfers planning for pars often make very few pars, some bogeys and a lot of others on those nemesis holes.

Re-evaluate the way you are going to play that nemesis hole the next time you face it. Create a game plan that will allow you play that hole more consistently. Avoid giving into the temptations to cut the corner and go for birdie. Play a 3 wood off the tee to a more safe location in the fairway. Lay-up if it will guarantee bogey and give you a shot to get up and down for par. Once you have reframed the way you are going to play the hole, go out and execute the plan until you get it right. Then you can attack other nemesis holes in the same manner. Eventually you'll be able to approach all your game plans more productively with a performance-oriented edge.

As you consider your new plan, evaluate what you need to do to make bogey. For example, on the average par four for men all you need to play is a 150 yard tee shot and 150 yard lay-up to leave a third shot of inside 100 yards. A position from which you can get up and down for par, or secure your bogey by playing a wedge on the green and two putting. So, your goal is to find a plan that guarantees you will reach par 4's in three strokes, then two putt. On par 5's the plan is to reach the green in four and two putt. If you apply this strategy for 18 holes you will score 90.

Lower handicap golfers may find this approach less than satisfying. If you already have a confident feel for your woods, or if you can commit to swinging your woods in a more controlled manner, while giving up a little distance, then you can try that approach. Get a scorecard from your home course. On the card I want you to make a mark on the holes you regularly have trouble playing. Circle par on those holes and replace it with one over par for each hole. On these holes, you are going to create a new game plan.

Your new game plan can include playing woods off the tee, just play a more controlled driver, or fairway wood. You may go as far as to imagine bunting your drives down the fairway. Whatever your choice, stick to one that guarantees you'll play to a safe location in the fairway, even if it is somewhat shorter off the tee than ideal. Then consider a lay-up option, one that will give you a good chance of getting up and down while guaranteeing bogey.

You may choose to play your approach shot right, left, short, or even long of the green. Pick a lay-up location that gives you a good angle to play your third shot toward a generous portion of the green. From there you can two putt for bogey. You may even one putt for par. The more you execute this game plan, the more often you will save par from the lay-up location, the more often you will secure bogey, and the less often you will score others. Give it a try, you'll be surprised. Now let's get back to reframing that nemesis hole with the evaluation chart on the next page.

# Performance-Oriented Evaluation Chart:

| Physical Skills | Game Plan | Inner Conviciton |
|---|---|---|
| *Skills Ready To Be Used* | *A Game Plan I Believe In* | *Total Absorption* |
| Imagine standing on the tee and assessing what shot you can confidently play into the fairway. Even if it means laying back further. | Consider your personal par on this hole and consider adjusting it to fit your confidence level. | Visualize each shot coming to rest in the chosen landing area. |
| Consider playing more down the right, left, or middle of the fairway to give you a better chance of keeping the ball in play. | Consider how far you really need to play your tee shot. | Imagine how the chosen action feels when performed well. |
| Consider playing a fairway wood, utility club or even an iron off the tee. | Consider what lay-up areas give you the best opportunity to score lower. | Clarify your performance routine and start the process. |
| Make a rehearsal swing to clarify if your club selection is truly a ready to use selection. | Consider what wedge distance you need to lay up to so you can confidently play your wedge to the green. | If unwanted thoughts pop-up clear your mind and start your routine over. |
| Notice how confident your rehearsal swing feels and assess its readiness. If there are any doubts, choose another action. | See each shot landing in a friendly location in the fairway. | Use relaxed breathing to re-establish a confident disposition before you restart your routine. |
| Be confident in your club selection. | Believe in your game plan. | Find your determination in your inner confidence. |
| Be confident in the chosen action. | Clarify each choice as you play each shot. | Trust the process to direct your performance. |
| Stay committed. | Stay committed | Stay Committed |

# Performance Routine:

*Once again, never forget these three steps of your Performance Routine.*

| Physical Skills | Game Plan | Inner Conviction |
|---|---|---|
| Always Choose Skills Ready To Be Used. You Can Only Perform What You've Prepared Yourself To Do. | Always Choose A Game Plan You Can Believe In. You Must Have Conviction Backing Up Your Choices. | Absorb All Your Attention, Focus, and Determination Into The Process. Then Trust The Process And React. |

You may wonder why I call it a performance routine instead of a pre-shot routine, or even a shot routine. There are a couple of reasons for choosing the term *"performance routine"* over "shot routine." The obvious reason is that thinking of the routine as a shot routine makes the shot, the result, more important than the performance. However, the performance must come first. It is impossible to perform the shot without executing the wing. What you perform is the cause, and the shot is the result of the performance.

The fact is, golfers who are more involved in a performance routine become more performance-oriented, and golfers involved in a shot routine become more result-oriented. You may say it is just semantics, but words have meaning and the more you use the words, the more disposed you are to act on them.

It's like hanging around the wrong crowd. The more you associate yourself with a group of people, the more you act like people in the group. So, the more you use the misleading words, the more you act on them. However, the more you use words that truly describe what you want to accomplish the more often you accomplish your goals.

Another reason I use performance routine is that a performance routine considers all the factors relating to your ongoing readiness to perform well. That means your performance routine considers the pre-shot decision making process, the during the swing action process, and the post-swing assessment and recommitment process. I hope it is obvious that pre-shot routines end when the swing starts, and shot routines end when the shot is completed. Neither one considers the assessment and recommitment part of the process. A truly complete performance routine considers the whole process.

Although the performance-routine was presented without the assessment and recommitment parts of your routine, they will need to be incorporated into the process. They are the post-swing steps, and they are important enough to have their own chapter, so we will discuss them in the next chapter. Steps 1 thru 3 guide you into the action portion of the performance mode, while assessment and recommitting support your ongoing preparation. When it is your turn to play, isolate the first three steps of the performance process. When your play is completed, switch your focus to assessment and recommit.

By now I hope it is obvious that your level of preparation will greatly influence your level of performance. However, even if you are prepared, your performance will suffer if you fail to stay performance-oriented.

That means you must be more committed to absorbing yourself into the process than you are considering the results. Being result conscious will create more doubts and indecision than you can overcome. Being performance-oriented will greatly reduce the unwanted thoughts and will help you stay more focus. As a matter of fact, the more absorbed you are in the performance routine, the less room there is for the unwanted thoughts to pop-up. In the end, the golfer who is able to be more decisive and committed in the process will be more performance-oriented.

# Chapter Seven
## *Recommitting: Staying The Course*

The main key to staying on course with your chosen game plan is being able to recommit. Recommitment is critical to holding yourself true to your chosen game plan. We all get side tracked, and it is easy to get down on ourselves when times are tough. It is easy to react emotionally to misguided efforts, and it is easy to lose heart when things fail to work out as planned.

One of the first things you need to realize is that it is impossible to be successful 100% of the time. For example, successful businessmen are considered extremely successful if they can close the deal 30% of the time. Scientists and researchers constantly experience setbacks. However, their efforts are still productive. What we call our failures are actually steps toward success. They let us know what works and what doesn't. We may perceive them as failures, but in reality they are simply efforts that awaken us to how things work.

Since it is likely that you will experience many setbacks as you go through life, you must be determined to recommit to the process once you've gotten sidetracked. Recommitting is a much more productive response than losing heart. Instead of losing heart, think like the scientist who tries, tries again without getting discouraged. Remember, your successful efforts will pay off big time, and with recommitment your successful efforts will show up more frequently.

Staying the course can be facilitated by reinventing yourself in the moment. You can quiet your mind, reframe your attitudes, reorganize your perceptions, regain your focus, and recommit to the vision of being the golfer you want to be. Do you remember that vision? The vision of a golfer that plays with etiquette and conducts himself with dignity. Can you visualize yourself as a golfer that maintains her commitments to the performance routine? Can you envision yourself staying the course of being performance-oriented? Can you envision yourself being this golfer? If so, recommit to it once you noticed you've been sidetracked.

Recommitment begins by quieting the mind, by emptying it of unwanted attitudes, emotions, and responses. Recommitment involves reinventing yourself by regaining your composure and by being determined to get back to your commitments as a golfer. Let's step back for a moment. Even though we all want to conduct ourselves with impeccable etiquette, we all know that we have our moments, we all have bad days. We all know that our emotions can get the best of us. We all react negatively at times. We are all human.

Even if our reactions are hidden behind the mask of a straight face, we all succumb to negativity from time to time. Of course, some golfers give in more frequently than others. So, because we are human beings, because we are bound to be guided off track from time to time, we must be ready to recommit to the process. We must be willing to recommit to a process that redirects our efforts and realigns our commitments to staying the course of being performance-oriented.

Understanding why we react negatively can help us break our negative patterns and make it easier to recommit to the process. The first thing to realize is that your reactive habits are conditioned, instead of inherent to your nature. These habits can be molded, influenced, and changed to be more positive and more productive.

Your preconditioned beliefs generate a storyline that makes you predisposed to react to the present conditions. Your preconditioned beliefs create your underlying disposition, and because of this disposition you are inclined to act in a preconditioned manner when presented with a certain set of circumstances. Given these circumstances, you are inclined to react the same way each time you encounter the given situation. Therefore, each time you buy into the storyline, you are inclined to react in a way that your negative attitudes and responses are ignited.

You can change your inclination to react negatively, you can change the disposition that allows you to buy into the story-line. You can change your attitudes and responses by changing the storyline you believe in. It's just a storyline, and if it's a bad one, you can drop it and write a new one; one with a positive outlook, one that is performance-oriented, and one that provides purpose to the activity.

We often get caught up in the storyline because we buy into concepts of right and wrong, good and bad, win and lose. All those concepts are mental considerations instead of awareness-based observations. And those considerations sprout opinions about what is happening, why it is happening, what is suppose to be happening, and what does it all mean. The woulda-shoulda-coulda's once again follow and the story-line becomes more captivating.

Throughout that process we forgot that performance was the goal, and performing the actions was the intention. So, because of our human tendencies, part of the performance-routine needs to consider how we can stay the course immediately after completing our shots. And if we get caught up in our emotions and mental tendencies during this post-swing period, we need to have a means of getting back into the game plan. When the performance is done, our attention needs to switch to openly assessing what happened, followed by getting back to being purposeful.

One of the best ways of combating your reactive habits is by making a real commitment to learn from your experiences, good or bad. Honoring such a commitment involves assessing how well you prepared yourself for the last swing, it also involves assessing how absorbed your focus was while swinging. The trouble is, it is impossible to clearly assess these considerations when you are reacting emotionally to the results. And you certainly have trouble understanding how your performance caused the results if you are reacting, complaining, and ruminating over the unwanted results.

Learning to be non-judgmental in your post-shot assessment will help you keep your disposition on course and will help keep things in perspective. Open awareness is a non-judgmental activity, and it is a process that provides information that will keep your assessments performance-oriented. The main benefit of open awareness is clarity. Clarity with regard to what actions occurred and clarity with regard to how those actions affected your performance.

It is unnecessary to analyze why the actions happened. However, it is necessary to notice how the actions influenced your performance.

Non-judgmental awareness is just noticing what's happening, noticing as if you are simply an observer, an observer who is emotionally detached from the situation. That means an observer who is able to report what actions occurred and what results followed. It means an observer who can observe without analyzing the whys, how comes, what ifs, and woulda-shoulda-coulda's. It also means, an observer who can simply be aware of what happened, instead of overanalyzing the situation.

As negative reactions occur, we also have a tendency to talk to ourselves negatively, and the more negatively you talk to yourself the harder it is to recommit to the process. Learning to talk to yourself in a more supportive manner can help you stay on course. While learning to talk to yourself positively, learn to eliminate habits of complaining, tendencies to put yourself down, and self criticism. Learning to compliment your efforts, learning to reward yourself for being successful, and learning to apply open awareness will help you stay the course without the frustrating roller coaster ride of emotional reactions and analytical detours.

Why are we so inclined to talk to ourselves negatively? Why do we find it so easy to talk ourselves away from our goals and our dreams? If other people talked to us the way we talk to ourselves, we'd call them enemies. However, we continue to listen to our self-talk as if it is good advice, offered by a valued advisor. I wonder, if a therapist, coach, or caddy talked to us in this way, would we continue to listen, or would we fire them?

Learn to be your own best friend, your own best coach, and your own best advisor! When a client gets side-tracked, a good therapist, coach, or caddy always remembers the chosen game plan, they are always concerned with keeping their client's activity focused toward the chosen goal. And when their client's emotions rise, they stay clear of the confusion while staying the course.

Being anchored in the commitment to stay the course makes it possible for them to calm their clients down, clear the slate, and refocus their efforts on the chosen course of action. As the golfer, you would be wise to become your own best therapist, your own best coach, and your own best caddy by learning to be more supportive in your self-talk, more aware in your observations, and more real in your assessments.

To further help you stay the course, you can commit to making the best out of every situation you encounter. Then, even your rough days will turn out productive. Keep in mind, performance and results sometimes fail to add up. Outside factors, ones out of your control, can influence the results. You can make a perfect swing, read all the conditions perfectly, then a gust of wind can come up and knock your ball out of the air and into a bunker. You did everything by the book, you performed through absorbed focus, and something happened that was out of your control. Choose to let it go, get back to the preparation process, recommit to the game plan, and go get the ball up and down out of the bunker. Ruminating over your bad luck will make it more difficult get up and down.

Staying the course also involves recommitting to the game plan in the middle of the round. When you get sidetracked you need to get back into the game. Just because you failed to execute the game plan perfectly, up to this point, does that mean you should bail on it? Get back into the game plan and notice you score better on the holes that follow the game plan compared to the ones that detour away from the plan. So, recommitting to the game plan will require that you clear your mind of self-talk and analysis. It will require being present, clarifying the process, and recommitting whole-heartedly.

In future chapters we will discuss better ways of clearing your mind and being present so you can more easily recommit to the process. For now, simply realize that recommitting is an integral part of a productive game plan. Remember, what led you off course is unimportant. The key is to recognize that you've become mental and now you need to clear your mind of its opinion based, story telling habits. The moment you recognize that you are caught up in the story-line, recommit to your chosen game plan. You simply need to get back into the game by dropping the story and recommitting to the game plan.

# Chapter Eight
## *Composure: Being Purposeful*

In past chapters we have discussed a lot about clarifying our choices, actions, and our commitments. We have discussed how our commitments hold us to our chosen way of being golfers. Now it is time to understand why we play golf in the first place. It is time to understand how to be purposeful in our play, and it is time to understand how being purposeful will bring about having composure. And with this final piece of the process in place, the golfer's edge can be realized.

Maintaining composure is a matter of having clarity, commitment, and purpose throughout the whole process. Clarity comes from knowing why you choose to play the game. Commitment is found because you know your reasons for playing are your own, and they are the right ones for you. If there is any doubt as to why you play the game, there will be a lack of commitment. Composure comes from having a bigger view of yourself, your game, and the purpose for being a golfer.

Clarity is facilitated by an open awareness, awareness that leads you to the choices that are ready to be made, and clarity allows you to choose a worthwhile purpose for playing the game. Commitment is solidified by unconditional confidence in yourself, the choices you make, and your reasons for playing. You can commit without question because your choices are right for you and because you are unconditionally confident in who you are. Win or lose you did your best, and you satisfied your purpose for playing.

Composure is maintained by being deeply rooted in the process, it is a choice to be so unwavering in your attitude towards every moment, and it is a choice to realize that your purpose for playing is more important than the results of the day.

Let's back track for a second. What considerations do we need to clarify? What are the important factors to isolate? An obvious consideration is clarifying a target to play toward. A less obvious consideration is clarifying your intentions, such as your purpose for playing the game. While clarifying these factors, try to recognize the underlying beliefs and attitudes that influence your behavior as you play your way around the course. It is especially important to recognize the underlying beliefs and attitudes that undermine your productive efforts. Your underlying beliefs and attitudes need to clarify your goals and your purpose for playing. With your beliefs, attitudes, goals, and intentions all in line, you can truly satisfy your purpose for playing golf.

Your main goal when playing golf is to score as low as you can, and you engage in this process by playing each shot to a target, one shot at a time. Off the tee, your target is a location in the fairway that leaves you a generous angle to the green. From the fairway, your target is a location on the green that leaves you a good opportunity to two putt . And once on the green, your goal is to roll the ball down the intended line and into the cup – the final destination of each hole.

Since your goal is to play a shot to the intended target, your intention must be to perform a swing that will play the ball down the intended line of flight to the target. Having the intention of merely hitting the ball is insufficient. In fact, giving into the intention of merely hitting the ball solidly will distract you from your true goal of delivering the ball to the target and the necessary intention of performing a swing that will get the job done.

A swing that sends the ball to a target location must possess throughness. A swing intending to hit the ball is merely ball bound. With this in mind, it ought to be obvious that without clarifying the goal to be target-oriented and the intention to perform an action that swings thru to the target, you will never be proficient at achieving your goals.

Once it is clear what your true goals and intentions are, you must take your commitments to a deeper level. True commitments come from having the conviction to trust your swing to deliver the ball to your intended target. If you are focused on the target and intend to trust your swing to send the ball to the target, then all you need to do is have the conviction to absolutely trust the process.

Your true intentions are the ones that actually direct your swings. What you wish, or desire is less important. What matters is what you truly intend to do, because what you truly intend to do shows up in your actions, and the precision of your actions shows you how much conviction you maintained. So, your truest intentions ought to focus on performing the actions that will achieve your goals. Your truest intentions ought to be performance-oriented. Are your true intentions performance-oriented?

When you make your rehearsal swings it is often the case that your intention is to feel as good a swing as possible. This is why most golfers feel they make beautiful practice swings. Then they approach the ball and intend to hit the ball solidly. In that moment they switched their intention from being performance-oriented to being result-oriented, and in the process the activity lost its purpose. So, put some purpose into your swings, give the swing the intention of being performance-oriented, give your swing the intention of delivering the shot to the target.

That is a simple view of intending to play your best golf, and it seems easy, however lots of undermining intentions are lurking, waiting to inhibit your purposeful intentions. As my coach Fred Shoemaker writes in *Extraordinary Golf,* "most golfers come to the first tee committed only to looking good (hitting a good shot) and not being embarrassed. This desire for others' approval is so basic that most golfers are not even aware of it. It is the medium in which they live, much like water for a fish and air for a bird. The fact that this desire is so common as to be unnoticeable makes it even more entrenched in the golfer's mind, and it can easily overpower other commitments that a golfer might try to have."

That passage expresses the type of underlying intentions that can undermine your purpose for playing golf. I hope it is obvious that such a perspective fails to be purposeful. So, be aware of your true intentions and notice how they influence your conviction to execute a performance-oriented and purposeful process.

Let's get back to being purposeful in our play. Is intending to be target-oriented while trying to score as low as possible really our purpose for playing the game? Or is there some other reason we have for playing? Scoring low is simply the goal of the game. It is simply one of the guidelines stated in the rules of the game. The goal is to play the course in as few a number of strokes as possible. Does that explain why we choose to play the game? I know for myself I fell in love with golf long before I ever had the pleasure of playing on the golf course. I got hooked when I was nine, the first time my dad took me to the driving range. I can still remember my first pure shot. I can see it flying directly in line with my intended target. The whole experience captured me. The feel of everything coming together, the look of the shot flying exactly how I intended it to fly, that was enough for me. It was another two years before I even stepped on a golf course.

In Japan, many people practice at driving ranges and never get to play golf. It is simply too expensive, or the opportunity to play at a course are few and far in between. I have taught many Japanese golfers that practiced regularly for up to six years without playing on a golf course. Was it the dream of scoring as low as possible that kept them going? Or was it the experience of it all coming together, one shot at a time? We make statements like, "That's the one that will keep me coming back for more." If that is true, then there must be something more to playing than simply scoring low. There must be some other purpose for playing. A purpose that warrants the type devotion we all give to the game.

This brings us to the question, "What type of game deserves your deepest conviction?" What purpose for playing the game can keep you motivated throughout the whole round? What purpose will keep your interest level high? What purpose will keep you fascinated and absorbed into the process? What purpose will keep you coming back for more? Simply trying to look good and avoid embarrassment lacks purpose. I know for myself, it will never keep me interested in doing my best.

For me, playing golf with a sense of composure and conducting myself in the vision of the warrior-competitor are purposes worth playing for. I also believe that committing to the purpose of enjoying myself is a worthwhile purpose for playing golf. Simply playing with the purpose to learn more about yourself is a worthwhile purpose. Learning to trust yourself with true conviction is a wonderful purpose for playing the game. There are many worthwhile purposes for playing golf. Spending time in nature, getting to know friends and family better, exercising, and learning how to stay genuine during the heat of competition are all wonderful purposes for playing.

The best purposes are the ones you choose freely, and they are the ones that inspire enjoyment and personal growth. If you think about it, you get to choose the purpose for playing golf. As stated, the rules of the game identify the goal of the game as scoring as low as possible while playing within the rules. Where in the rules does it state why you should play the game? Why you play is up to you, and why you play is your purpose for playing.

Most purposes for playing the game can be served during the in between shot periods on the golf course. If you think about it, you spend more time in between shots than you do playing shots. An 18 hole round of golf provides you over 3 1/2 hours of time to satisfy your chosen purpose for playing. You get less than an hour to score well. Whether the purpose is enjoying the course's natural setting, whether it is getting to know your playing partners better, whether it is to conduct business, or whether it is engaging in self growth, you can serve the purpose in between shots.

Managing this process involves switching your focus from satisfying your performance routine to satisfying the purpose for playing. I call that process "flipping the switch." Throughout your performance routine you are concerned with clarifying your targets, choosing ready to use actions, applying your intentions with true conviction, and responding to your play with composure.

When the performance routine is completed, you must flip the switch to attending to your chosen purpose for the day. Finishing your performance routine with composure will make it easy to flip the switch to being purposeful in between shots. However, when you lose your composure, becoming emotional and mental, it becomes difficult to give true conviction to being purposeful.

When you can flip the switch to being purposeful in between shots, your golf becomes much more enjoyable and fulfilling. It also makes it easier to get back into your performance routine when it is your turn to play. If you undermine your purpose for playing by ruminating on your bad luck, complaining about your missed shots, or venting your emotions in between shots, it will become very difficult to switch your focus back to the performance routine when it is your turn to play.

This reminds me of other situations in sports such as icing a player on the free throw line in basketball, calling a timeout in football right before the snap of the ball on a field goal attempt, and waiting to serve in tennis. Why do they call time outs during those critical moments in basketball and football?

Opposing teams call timeouts because they hope the free throw shooter or kickers will use the timeout to think about what they are going to do. They know if they can get the player thinking about it, then the player will become mental and he'll have a good chance of missing the shot. What happens to a tennis player when they are serving poorly. They think too much about it, they become mental. In each case the player is way more concerned with results then satisfying their purpose for playing the game.

Purposeful performers fill their downtime with purposeful activities. When the timeout is called, the key player relaxes and returns ready to fulfill his chosen purpose. If the player is a fun loving person, then she can try joking with her teammates, or the crowd. If the player loves being in the spotlight, he can look through the crowd and notice how much energy is being sent his way. If the player simply loves the game, she can enjoy the moment and soak it all in.

During these down times it is much more valuable to occupy your time satisfying your purpose for the game than it is becoming mental. If I was a team coach that had players who needed to get through these periods of down time I would have each player write down reasons why they love to play the game. Then I would have each player write down a purpose they can happily serve during timeouts designed for icing the player. Then I'd have each player rehearse performing these purposeful activities. The more they rehearse, the more often they will get through the critical down times without becoming mental. The result will be better performance when it comes time to play.

Committing to a purpose will make your game purposeful. Purposeful activity will keep your perspective positive, and will help you maintain composure. So being purposeful in between shots and composed during your performance routine will keep the whole golfing activity positive. This will certainly create a sound foundation for scoring well, enjoying your play, and creating the golfer's edge.

As I stated earlier, composure is maintained by being deeply rooted in the process, it is a choice to be unwavering in your attitude toward every moment of your play, and it's a choice to maintain such a sense of purpose.

If you have a clear and committed performance routine, and a clear and committed choice to satisfy a purpose, you will certainly play with composure. Maintaining such a process is an achievement you can be proud of, and one that has a good chance of keeping your interest alive.

# Part Three
## *Keeping The Process Fertile*

# Chapter Nine
## *Mindfulness: Monitoring the Patterns*

Mindfulness is the practice of cultivating our different modes of awareness. There are three main modes of awareness: passive awareness, active awareness, and spacious awareness. In each mode of awareness the individual is cultivating his ability to be attentive in the present. Thoughts, storylines, and mental chatter distract us from being present. They lure us into the past and future. They trap us with expectations and judgments, and they confuse us with rationalizations and justifications. The fog of cluttered thought patterns make it impossible to be aware of the present needs. They make focus problematic, and being purposeful unlikely.

So, the first step of being mindful is to understand the nature of our attentiveness. What are we attending to? Is it the random thought streams that run through our minds, the environmental stimuli presented in the moment, a chosen focal point within our present situation, or an expanding awareness of the space we live within?

The main thing to remember here is, all modes of being mental are what can be called daydreaming states, they pull us out of our present state of awareness and throw us into a world of mental consideration. Conversely, all states of awareness are present in nature, they absorb us into an attentive medium whose mechanisms are sensory in origin.

The medium of the mind is mentality through thought. The medium of awareness is attentiveness through sensory feedback. The mentality of thought always has a story-line foundation. The storyline may pertain to reality or it may be based in fantasy. Attentiveness through sensory feedback is by its nature a present activity, and its baseline is reality.

The benefits of the mind-mentality-thought processes are creativity, organization, and choice. The benefits of the awareness-attentiveness-sensory processes are performance, observation, and experience.

Applied to golf, the mind is most valuable in the activities of understanding course management and course design. That includes knowing what clubs to use from which yardages, knowing which shots fit the given situation, knowing which options fit your normal mode of playing, and making choices that fit these considerations. Additionally, the activities of the mind are well suited for organizing and establishing a plan for improvement. During the improvement process, the activities of the mind are suited for remembering and categorizing the information that helps you stay the course of improvement.

Applied to golf, awareness is used most valuably in the activities of focus and absorption. Since focus and absorption are the main vehicles of performance, awareness is the main vehicle of your performance routine. Therefore, when performance is the goal, the task becomes using awareness to absorb yourself into the focus that will get the job done, and this process is organized into your performance routine. This makes awareness the medium in which you experience performance.

Awareness is also valuable in the learning process. As far as learning is concerned, awareness allows you to recognize what experiences get the job done. You might say, awareness allows you to observe the patterns of the physical world.

As you may now gather, the more you are engaged in mental activity, the more you will be caught up in the story-line, and being caught up in the story-line will lead you to mental considerations such as doubts, fears, and expectations. Conversely, the more time you spend being aware of the present conditions, the more likely you will be attentive to the needs that will get the job done, and that will allow you to seize your opportunities and enjoy quality performance. Therefore, it is very useful to be able to distinguish the difference between being mental and being aware, and that is the task of mindfulness.

When you can distinguish the differences between your mental modes of being and your awareness modes of being, you will truly understand the difference between being an academic and being a performer. Performers act, react, and do things through the medium of awareness. Academic's think, analyze, and organize thru the medium of mentality. And although our academic prowess may give us an edge in scholarly endeavors, it can make us too mental when it comes to performance. Whereas awareness by its nature, will always bring us into the light of our present reality.

So once again, being intellectual may have its place, but when performance is the goal, it needs to be set aside for awareness. I've often heard golfers say, "You either need to be a genius or an absolute idiot to play great golf." Additionally, while playing professional golf I've heard many players call themselves, "mental midgets." These comments seem to point to the intellectual level of the golfer, and they allude to the idea that being a little intelligent is problematic for the golfer. In one case, the less mentally inclined you are, the better you play. In another, you need to be smart enough to know when to turn the smarts off.

For example, the idiot has little concern for being intellectual. His only pretense is being himself, so he simply is aware of what's going on around him and he reacts to the given situation naturally. When things go astray he simply laughs them off, accepts that it is what it is, and gets back to the drawing board in hopes of improving. Then on occasions when everything is dialed in, his performance is elevated, and he simply enjoys the moment. Sounds like a pretty smart approach to playing actually, maybe more people would benefit from such an attitude.

The genius is studied in the art of the game. She has figured out the intricacies of her best techniques, knows her tendencies under pressure, has devised a performance-oriented game plan, then turns over the task of performance to being aware instead of being academic. The genius knows how to put her intellectualism aside and give complete trust to the processes of awareness. This also seems like an effective approach to playing.

The fact is, the so-called idiot is simply a person that is more concerned with being present and fun loving as compared to being studious, and that is his genuine nature. The so called genius may simply be curious as well as studious, but understands that being so has little to do with being a good performer. So she studies to become more knowledgeable and she trusts her awareness to guide her through performance. She simply has her priorities in perspective.

Additionally, the so-called "mental midget" has simply confused the modes of being and has yet to learn the value of prioritizing them. This person often has the pretense that being intelligent is the most important thing in life. This person is often strong-minded and less absorbed into the now. It is often because of the pretenses to be intelligent and strong minded that the mind continues to disrupt the awareness mode. Remember, a pretense is a conditioned state. Babies are born into the world without such pretense. However, all babies are born into the world with their faculties of awareness wide open, ready to receive whatever the world has to offer. Thus, every golfer would be wise to put aside their pretenses and learn to put things in perspective by prioritizing the mental activities for learning, organizing, and choosing the courses of action that will get the job done. Then they can prioritize the awareness activities for physical actions, observation, and experience.

So, once again, mindfulness is about distinguishing the difference between being mental and being aware. The basic practices of mindfulness are designed to help you understand how you use your mind and what you fill your mind with. When you fill your mind with thoughts, your mind is full of storylines, illusions, and ideas. When you fill your mind with awareness, your mind is attentive, observant, and full of reality. What do you fill your mind with on the golf course, and which way works best for performance?

There are mindful practices that help distinguish the difference between passive awareness and being mental. There are mindful practices that help distinguish the difference between active awareness and being mental, and there are mindful practices for distinguishing the difference between spacious awareness and being mental. So, let's describe what passive, active, and spacious awareness are, then we can get into some mindful practices.

Passive awareness is a process of open observation. The goal of passive awareness is to be aware of what your senses are receiving without thinking about what you are experiencing. The practices of passive awareness often involve being still and quieting the mind. Most basic meditation techniques involve passive awareness. These meditative practices involve sitting still in an upright posture, with eyes closed, while being mindful of your breathing pattern. While being mindful of your breath, you are to notice when thoughts pop in and distract you from the mindful activity of being aware of your breathing pattern.

Being mindful in this manner involves the mere observation of how you are breathing. Analyzing how well you are breathing would disrupt the process, and attempting to control the pattern of your breathing would make the process more mental as well. While observing the pattern of your breath, it is likely that random thoughts will pop in and visit your mind. When your mind gets stuck on a thought stream, the goal becomes to quiet the thoughts by getting back to the mindful practice of attending to the pattern of your breath. You quiet the mind by letting go of the thoughts as freely as they popped in. When the thought visitors persist, you can acknowledge their presence and simply ask them to leave with the next outgoing breath.

Passive awareness can be cultivated by simply noticing what your attention wanders to as well. Once again, while sitting still with your eyes closed, in an upright posture, you can begin noticing your breath. When your ears pick up sounds you will notice the sounds. The key is to notice them without getting stuck in thought about what it was and who made it. As freely as the sounds were noticed, let your attention move to the next stimuli. Maybe it is another sound, maybe it is a feeling, a taste, or a smell. Whatever stimuli you are attentive to, let it go as quickly as it came into your attention, and freely accept the next experience that intercepts your senses. Remember, the task here is to be attentive of whatever stimuli your sensory system picks up on from moment to moment.

In the beginning stages of mindful practice intellectuals often question, "Why am I doing this? I'm unsure of what I'm supposed to get out of this." This is simply the academic's conditioned habit to try and figure things out before they simply show up. However, mindful learning works on the premise of "ah-ha!" The "ah-ha" premise is the state of learning where you simply continue to observe without the inclination to figure anything out, then "ah-ha," something shows up and you understand how things work. Academics have trouble giving into this process because they have the pretense that the intellect is more important than being aware. They believe they can use the intellect to speed up the learning process. They believe intellectualism is a higher state of being than being present. Therefore, they strive to live most of their lives in the illusion of academia, instead of the reality of awareness. To that end intellectuals engage in mind games, whereas the so-called simple people believe in "ah-ha!"

Maybe there is another form of intelligence working behind the awareness process, and maybe the "ah-ha" experience is the expression of this hidden form of intelligence. Maybe we benefit most from using the intellect when it is most needed, and maybe we benefit from using awareness when it is most valuable. I think we would all benefit from prioritizing our modes of being in this manner.

Throughout your mindful practices, your mind will continually want to engage in some type of storyline. The storyline might be about the sensations you are experiencing, or they may be random thought streams that visit your accepting mentality. Whatever the case, they will distract you away from being attentive. Whenever you notice the thoughts linking into a storyline, you can quiet them by switching your focus back to being aware of your present sensory activity. Once again, the goal of passive awareness is to observe what engages your senses from moment to moment without thoughts distracting you from being attentive.

I often used passive awareness as I lay in bed waiting to fall asleep. I notice when I am simply being aware of my sensations from moment to moment without thoughts interfering with the process. When I can stay attentive I often fall quickly into a deep sleep. This is much like when you feel so exhausted you simply feel the feelings of exhaustion and fall asleep without thought streams keeping your attention awake. However, when thought streams invade my mind and persist, I can lay awake for hours without any hope of falling asleep.

When I wake up in the morning, I also like to begin my day with mindfulness of passive awareness. So, I lay in bed with my eyes closed, tune into my breath, and ride the flow of sensations that stimulate my being attentive. This type of practice allows me to begin each day anew. It allows me to start each day with clarity, purpose, and perspective. It allows me to begin each day without the clutter of unwanted storylines and left over confusion from days past. Indeed, whenever I feel imprisoned by habitual thought patterns I return to passive awareness. Through this practice I clarify the moment, regain presence, and restart my efforts with purpose. One of the great benefits of this training is that it opens your senses. When you open them in this manner you are exercising their fitness, you are exercising their readiness for use in your performance routine. So, passive awareness is the experience of being openly attentive to the sensitivity of your body, and mindfulness of passive awareness is the task of noticing how often thoughts interfere with the process.

Active awareness can be trained in much the same way as passive awareness. However, it has a chosen focal point to stay attentive to. The chosen focal point is one beyond simple observation. The chosen focal point is one you can imagine in your mind's eye, and the goal is to sustain the image as long as possible. Of course, the image will fade, and random thoughts will once again invade your attentive state of awareness. Even being passively aware of sounds and feelings will pull you out of your absorption into the image. When that happens, your goal is to re-imagine the image in your mind's eye and to stay as absorbed into the image as possible.

One of the great benefits of active awareness is strengthening your ability to stay focused on a chosen course of action. It is active awareness because it involves activating a choice and staying attentive to the choice. And that is exactly what you need to do when you make a choice to play golf. Shot after shot, from tee to green, from hole to hole, all the way around the course you must choose courses of action and attend to them if you are going to achieve your goal of performing well.

This is much like what you do when you drive your car. You are driving your car because you need to get somewhere. You choose a route that will get you to your destination in a timely manner, then you set out to drive to your destination. If you get caught up in thoughts while you are driving, you may veer into other lanes, or you may even miss your turn. Do you have these miscues because you are a bad driver? Or is it because you simply stopped attending to the task of driving and allowed your mind to wander? You gave into your mental tendencies. You became mental. As easily and as often as this happens when driving, it can happen on the golf course. Because, there is just as much room for letting your mind wander on the golf course as there is to let it wander while driving your car.

Active awareness is also important for attending to your chosen purpose. Since your purpose for playing is a choice you must actively engage in the choice if you are going to be purposeful. Simply riding the waves of passive attentiveness is insufficient for getting the job done. You must actively attend to the chosen purpose if you are going to satisfy the purpose. Whatever you are doing, if it involves choice then it requires being actively attentive. The involuntary functions of your body will continue to work, however directions are still needed to keep us on-track with our choices. Even walking is triggered by choice and must be attended to, otherwise you will walk into things or you will walk off the chosen course.

This brings us to the link between intention and attending to the chosen course of action. The only way you can experience what you intend to do is by being attentive to the concerns of your intention. Well, there is one other way, blind luck. However, if you truly intend to do something, then you will be attentive to the concerns that will bring your intentions alive. You will attend to the concerns that will produce the activity necessary to achieve your goals. Thus, intention without attentiveness is simply wishing, instead of true intention. In this way, active awareness is the task of being attentive to the concerns of what you intend to do. And mindfulness of active awareness is the practice of noticing how often your thoughts interrupt the process of attending to your chosen intention.

The type of attentiveness we develop through mindfulness of active awareness is the type of attentiveness we use for focus in sports. It is largely an inner eye process that brings together the intentions behind our choices with the sensory knowledge of our bodies. Once the inner eye image is programmed, all we have to do is stay attentive and the image will trigger the desired actions. To perform well, this process must be attended to with as little mental interference as possible if we are going to achieve high levels of focus.

Spacious awareness is trained much like passive awareness. It begins with the same routine of establishing an upright posture and being attentive to your breath. As you find yourself settling into the breath, open your attention to the sensations of your body. As you become more and more absorbed into the path of passive awareness, allow your attention to flow into your surrounding environment. With each outgoing breath allow your attention to expand into the spacious area surrounding you. As you continue, you allow your attention to expand farther and farther out into the world. Let it expand beyond the room you are sitting in. Let it expand beyond the building you live in. Let it expand beyond the neighborhood and city limits. Let it expand across the state and country, around the world, and out into space. Let it fill the boundaries of our universe and the expanding limits of the cosmos.

Staying attentive to your breath will keep you present, attending to your intentions will keep you performance-oriented, and expanding your attention throughout the space we live in will open your awareness to a bigger view of life. That is the goal of spacious awareness, awakening us to a more universal view of life. Spacious awareness opens our perception to the fact that we are simply a part of the cosmos, a very tiny part of the cosmos we live in. Being aware of how small a role each of us plays in relation to the rest of the world helps us keep things in perspective. Even so, our lives are still very important, because we indeed impact the other people in our lives. However, in relation to the whole cosmos, each of us is simply a speck in the whole scheme of things.

Let's entertain a situation where such understanding can be extremely valuable. Say you are in the middle of a round of golf, and you are playing exceptionally well. You tee off on the 15th hole, playing the ball down the right side of the fairway. You park your cart on the cart path on the left side of the hole, choose some clubs, and walk to the ball. When you get there you realize you've got every club but the one you need. Now the internal dialogue starts. You decide to use one of the clubs you have instead of walking back to the cart to get the correct one. It fails to work, and the situation continues to escalate until you finish the hole with a triple-bogey. Now you are fuming, complaining, and kicking yourself for being lazy. Then you finish the round all caught up in a storyline about how you ruined the best round of golf you were ever playing.

That attitude is a completely small-minded view of the game. Even the concept that the worst day on the golf course is better than the worst day at work is a bigger view of life. We often act like we are the center of the universe, and that everything important revolves around us. We often act like our present mishaps are the absolute worst things happening in the world. We often act like the mishaps of the moment are the worst things that have ever happened in our whole lives, they may even be the worst things that will ever happen to us, right? We act as if the rest of the world cares what's happening to us right now.

The fact is, there are car accidents, earthquakes, robberies, and much more terrible happenings occurring around the world right now. People are being devastated by deaths in the family, stock market crashes, and news of cancer. Other people are having babies, and making deals of a lifetime. And I'm pretty sure they can all careless that you were too lazy to walk back to the cart and get the club you needed. So put it in perspective. Good round or bad, your family will still be your family when you get home. You'll still have a roof over your head and food on the table. The outcome of the game will be just the outcome of the game. You still have a bright future. So, attend to keeping the game purposeful and in perspective?

The practice of spacious awareness reminds me of those posters from the 1970's. The ones that center on a city corner, with people walking the streets and views of what is going on in many of the apartments along the streets. The point of the poster is to open your mind to a bigger view of the world. It does so by depicting scenes of life throughout the poster. In one apartment, a newborn baby is being cherished by the lucky parents, through another window we see a man being attended to by paramedics. Down an alley we see someone being robbed, and on another street we see a child riding a bike for the first time. In another apartment we see a group of friends gathered playing games, and next door, someone committed suicide in the bathtub. Down the block a high school athlete is coming home with a trophy as his father is being arrested by the police. The poster is full of different types of life situations, and anyone of them could be your reality right now.

So, ask yourself, if choosing the wrong club is the worst thing that happens to you today, can you live with it? If making bogey, double bogey, or even quadruple bogey was the worst thing to happen to you today, can you live with it? Whenever a mishap happens, take a more expansive view of life and ask yourself to put the present situation in perspective.

Let's get back to the 15th hole. When you got to the ball and realized you needed a different club, you acted like the cart was on the other side of the known universe. You acted like it would be too much trouble to go back and get the club. Of course we make excuses like, "I'm going to slow up play," or "I'm going to make the group behind us mad." These are the most lame excuses we can come up with. Because, if our playing partners, or the group behind us, get upset because they have such a small minded view of the game, then they deserve to get upset. It is their choice, and they have to live with it. They caused themselves to get upset. They bought into the concept that it is a problem for a person to make a mistake and have to go back and get a different club. What, are they perfect? They've never done the same thing?

Additionally, if you choose to play with one of the clubs you had with you, then act responsibly and lay-up, or play to the right, left, or long of the green, whichever is safest and gives you the best chance to get up and down. You can even choke down on one club too much. Get creative. Avoid getting caught up in the storyline, followed by poor play, complaining, and acting like the whole universe is crumbling down on you. Make a choice you can live with and view it in the context of expansive awareness.

Why does it always take a tragedy, life-threatening situation, or natural disaster to plunge us into a more expansive view of our lives? Can it be because we become complacent in our lives? Can it be that we take for granted the relative safety of our society? Can it be we'd rather view our life situation as the center of the universe instead of view it as a microscopic speck of the cosmos? Whatever the reason, I believe we can all benefit from a more expansive view of our place in the world, and I believe we can all benefit from spacious awareness. It just might help you keep things in perspective the next time you are ready to lose your cool.

In review, mindfulness is the practice of cultivating your modes of awareness while noticing how often mental interferences get in the way of being present. Remember, all interferences occur when we become mental. Simply put, thoughts get in the way of our being present. And the thoughts we get stuck on distract us from performing the tasks we want to perform. To strengthen our powers of focus and reduce the occurrence of mental interference we can use mindfulness of passive awareness, mindfulness of active awareness, and mindfulness of spacious awareness.

Passive awareness will help strengthen the awareness capacities of your sensory system, active awareness will train you to more readily use awareness in your performance routine, and spacious awareness will be used to create a bigger mind perspective of the world and life.

In the next chapter we will further discuss the process of imagery and how it is used as an active awareness process to direct your performances. Then in chapter eleven I will introduce exercises that will help you further strengthen your ability to focus on being performance-oriented.

# Chapter Ten
## Imagery: The Perspective of Performance

Imagery is the perspective of performance because imagery activates our intentions into a state of awareness. Thus imagery is a medium, or vehicle, of active awareness. We use imagery awareness in our performance routine to formulate the intent of our choices into an awareness mechanism. And as we activate this programming, we are absorbing ourselves into an awareness mode that can be used to direct performance.

We use the resources of our inner eye to gather the physical and visual information necessary to create the image that will program and trigger the actions necessary to achieve our performance goals. Imagery is the mechanism of the inner eye, and imagery is the union of visualization and sensitivity. The thinking mind can visualize what we want to accomplish, however it incapable of trigging the body into action. It can only think about what we want to do and entertain stories that relate to our intentions. The body can both feel and perform the actions that will get the job done, however the body needs something to trigger the actions. It also needs something to formulate the intent of the actions.

There must be a meeting of the mind's intention and the body's actions if we are going to perform the necessary skills. This meeting of mind and body must be completed without mental interferences interrupting the process. The meeting must be such a complete integration that neither visualization nor feeling exist independent of each other. That is the task of active awareness, its conductor is the inner eye, and the medium is imagery.

Revisit the situation of driving a car. When you went about choosing the route you would take to get to your destination, did you imagine the route? Close your eyes for a moment. Pick a destination and decide on a route that will get you there. Did you imagine the destination, did you imagine what roads you'd travel, and did you imagine what turns you'd make to get to the destination? Some people even imagine how many stops they will have to make and adjust the route to minimize the number of stop signs and stop lights along the way.

When you play a well-executed lob shot over a bunker, do you imagine cutting under the ball and popping it up in the air? Do you imagine the ball landing softly without roll? Do you imagine the ball nestling up next to the hole? When you need to play the ball over a tree, do you imagine swinging thru the ball to create more lift? When playing bunker shots do you imagine splashing the sand and ball out of the bunker? When putting do you imagine the line of the putt and rolling the ball down the line? Do you imagine the ball falling in the hole? Do you imagine the sound of the ball rattling around in the cup? Accomplished players do.

The average player argues, "I'm unsure how to imagine those things." That's because you need to exercise imagery awareness if you are going to use it regularly. Little children are great at imagining things. They imagine things all day long. For some children, most of their waking hours are spent imagining whatever they can dream up. So, I have to believe that you had the skill at one point.

When you were born, you were born aware, fully engaged in passive awareness. It was your basic medium of life. As you became a child that realized a self-image, you developed a stronger sense of awareness. The sense of awareness was active awareness, or imagery awareness. You were born with the ability to imagine things. It was natural. It was part of your natural development as a human being. Children simply imagine how to do things because it is fun. As you were growing into an adult, you developed your intellect through academic practices in school. Those practices included mathematics, deduction, reasoning, and analytical thinking. Some of those practices develop naturally as well. Such as the little stories and white lies children tell so they can stay out of trouble. They pick those practices up through observation of how others act in their society.

At some point you stopped using your imagination as a mechanism for playing games, or maybe you simply limited the amount of imagination playing you allowed yourself to have. Maybe you justified it as growing up. Funny thing is, children are better at playing than adults, and adults are better at thinking than children. Children forget the negatives easily, adults remember them forever. Children need to be punished to entertain negativity, adults need to let go to have fun. By the time you become an adult, you entertain negativity regularly. Children need to be conditioned to think before they act, adults over do it.

Maybe we would all benefit from taking a lesson from children. Absorb yourself in awareness to learn about the world, imagine what you want to do, then act it out for performance.

We often hear great players, like Tiger Woods, say they love the short game and trouble shots because they require more imagination than the standard full shot. As we watch them play these shots, we are amazed when they seem to pull off the impossible. However, to those golfers, they see it as very possible. They were able to imagine it with a high degree of confidence, so they knew they could do it. Phil Mickelson is famous for expressing this mind-set, and he pulls off the seemingly impossible more often than most.

Of course, some may argue that he attempts those types of shots too often. So, he is criticized for playing that way. Then again, Arnold Palmer and Seve Ballesteros were praised for playing in such a go-for-broke manner. Arnold Palmer said the game is more fun playing that way. The point is, the times these players pulled off the improbable, their imagery was strong, their confidence was high, their conviction was true, and the whole process started with the inner eye creating an image they could believe in.

Great performers in all walks of life often talk about how they simply imagined what they needed to do, then did it. They describe being in the zone, the zone being a fluid state of imagery followed by action. You rarely hear a performer talking about how they thought their way through a great performance. Nor do they talk a lot about doubts, fears, and expectations. However, when they perform poorly, they often talk about being mental. They talk about having doubts, fears, and expectations that got in the way of their focus. In the end they conclude, "I just didn't have it today."

What was it they needed to have that day? Was it the talent or skill? I doubt it. Was it that they needed to be more prepared? Probably! Was it they were distracted by mental considerations? Most likely! Was it that they were unable to clearly and confidently imagine what they needed to do? Absolutely! Maybe they were preoccupied, maybe they failed to believe enough in their preparation, maybe their awareness pathways were being interfered with by mental chatter. Whatever the case, they were most likely unable to create the imagery awareness needed to trigger the necessary actions. They were most likely caught up in a storyline and detached from the present activity of being actively aware.

The fact is, most athletes rely on their talents and athleticism to carry them through their performances. They rely on the good days and weather the bad days. The best athletes know how to prepare themselves for the task. The best athletes know how to use their inner eye to direct performance. You, too, would benefit greatly from learning how to cultivate the strength of your inner eye imagery.

I hope it is clear that without the ability to imagine what you want to do achieving consistency in your performances will be problematic. Imagining what you want to do is the perspective you need to have before you engage in performing the task. The more clear your perspective, the stronger the perspective, and the more committed you are to absorbing yourself into the perspective of performance, the better the chance you have of performing well.

The intellectual spends most of his time cultivating the mind, and can therefore often visualize what he wants to do. However, the intellectual spends too little time feeling his body actions, and therefore has a hard time putting his thoughts into action.

The average athlete spends most of her time conditioning herself to play the game, however, often neglects the organization to excel. Top performers condition their minds and bodies for the task of performance and in doing so they learn to use their inner eye imagery to bring together the efforts of their physical training with their mental organization. So, when you want to perform well, absorb yourself into an inner eye image that satisfies the task you want to complete. Absorb yourself into the image as if you are diving into a swimming pool of imagery. Get yourself completely wet with imagery. Even better yet, absorb yourself into the image like a sponge in a big pool of water. Learn to absorb yourself so fully into the image that you are both surrounded by the image and feel the image flowing through you.

Remember the task of the actress. The actress learns all she can about the role to be played. She learns so much about the role, the setting, the background of the era, and all the nuances of the character she will play. As she absorbs herself into the outside influences of the role she begins to feel as if she really is in the environment of the character. Then she goes a step further, by soaking up the known feelings, emotions, and attitudes of the character. The more she soaks up, the more she acquires the character's mind-set, habits, and tendencies. As the character's inner qualities become absorbed into the actress, the actress becomes the character because she is imagining everything that pertains to being the character. As you can imagine, that process takes a lot of imagination. It interests me that actors and actresses are performers. They are just as much performers as athletes, and athletes are like actors in that they act out the role of being a player in the game of choice.

So, just like fish swimming in the medium of water, birds flying in the medium of air, and planets existing in the medium of space, performers perform through the medium of imagery. Sounds great, but how am I going to do that you ask? In the next chapter I will introduce exercises for better performance, and some of these exercises will involve strengthening your inner eye processes for the task of active awareness.

# Chapter Eleven
## *Focusing: Better Performance Exercises*

Now that you have the whole process in perspective you are ready to develop the focus that will produce better performance, and part of that process will involve developing the use of your inner eye. Your inner eye is the eye of your inner golfer. I know this concept might sound abstract. So I am going to give you exercises to help you experience how this works. For now, consider the possibility that your inner golfer sees through your inner eye, and the mode of vision your inner eye uses is imagery.

We all know we need to focus in order to play well. But what is focus and where does it come from? Furthermore, what is the specific type of focus you need to play golf? Earlier in the book I stated that imagery is an application of active-awareness. So what is imagery, and how do we use it actively. Imagery is a process in which your inner eye captures the look and the feel of a given activity. The process of imagery is a creative process, and the actions we perform through imagery are artistic in nature. Therefore, the process of imagery is much more an intuitive activity than it is a thinking process.

Consider also that playing golf is a creative process. Just like a painter expresses the images of his inner being through the strokes of his brush, the golfer expresses his inner desires through the strokes of his club. Both activities express our inner creativity, so both actions are artistic. All artists imagine, and what they imagine, they express in their art. The fact is, the artist has a real image to express.

The key point here is that the image is real. It is real because it is an expression of the artist's inner being. Since it is **of** the inner being, it *"is"*, which makes it real. In other words, the artist is expressing something that is real, and it was experienced through imagery. So, what's the difference between imagery and fantasy? I believe that images have a real connexion with our being alive. They are connected to our experience through awareness. More so, they are an expression of what we are aware of. Fantasies, on the other hand, fail to have a real connexion to our world. Fantasies are the product of the thinking mind, and although they may be a type of creation, they fail to give birth to real experience.

Images have, as an integral part, sensitivity, and it is this sensitivity that connects us to the now, to the real. So, images are a projection of our possible realities, and they are based on the awareness we have acquired through our experiences. The mental storylines we create in our minds are fantasies. They may be exciting fantasies, sad fantasies, fearful or anxious fantasies. They may be frustrating fantasies, or any other type of fantasy you can think up, but they are just fantasies.

My coach, Fred Shoemaker, expresses this point quite clearly. In his book *Extraordinary Golf - The Art of the Possible*, he writes, "There is a difference between possibilities and fantasies, and I think we all know what the difference is. Real possibilities inspire us to action, while fantasies tend to make us mere dreamers. If a future has real possibility, it pulls us toward it. If it is just fantasy, it has no real connection with us. If a future truly enlivens and inspires us, then it is the right one."

I believe fantasies happen in the thinking brain, just like mathematics do. To me mathematics is as much fantasy as a dream is. It is just as abstract as our dreams. Deduction and reason are also types of fantasy. They may describe what happens, or what happened. Yet they are still just theories. Logic is the fantasy of the reasoning mind. Just as the types of fantasies you can have are unlimited, so are the types of scenarios you can produce with the thinking mind. Such mental stories are truly fantasy. They fail to keep open the real possibilities that exist for your future. I believe it is imperative to become aware of the distinction between the two, for the type of focus that will enrich your life has a connexion to you, to your experience. It has real possibility that can be expressed through action. So, the reality is in your experience, and fantasy is in your thoughts.

Experience is a mighty teacher. It can teach us to have faith in what we are unable to explain, yet know inwardly to be true. So listen to your inner golfer and try to see the wisdom it provides you. Therefore, I challenge you to take the journey inward, to seek the expressions your inner golfer provides you. I challenge you to focus in on the images you see in your inner eye, and I challenge you to use your inner eye to imagine what it is your inner golfer desires to express.

Consider the possibility that the appropriate images are already provided for you. You simply need to recognize them. These images are provided by your inner golfer, and your inner golfer wants you to express them outwardly. As you look at your present situation on the golf course, your eyes send visual feedback to your inner golfer. Your body also sends kinesthetic information to your inner golfer.

As your inner golfer receives that information, it formulates an image of the best way to approach the situation.

As your inner golfer formulates the image, it provides it for your use. All you have to do is to acknowledge its presence. You can experience that image with your inner eye if you want. When you find it hard to tap into the images, you can ask your inner golfer for some advice. You might be surprised to find that your inner golfer is dying to get into the game. It is enthusiastic about passing the appropriate image on to your present awareness.

When you find it hard to get in tune with your inner images, it's quite often the case that you are stuck in mental distraction. As you become consumed with mental storylines, you are stuck in a thinking mode, and you are unable to acknowledge the inner eye images. Therefore, you must find a way to let your mental storylines go. You must pass them back to the fantasy world, get back to the now. One good way of doing this is to close your eyes and exercise switching your attention between a thinking process, and an imagery process. That process is a sort of meditation drill. You can do the drill anywhere, even without a club or a ball, all you need is your imagination.

Find a comfortable place to sit, one that's quiet and will have minimal outside distractions. Once you've executed the exercise for a while, you'll be able to do it anywhere, even in the busiest airport. The goal of the drill is to help you understand the distinction between thinking with your conscious mind, and imagining with your inner eye. Once you've located a comfortable location, settle into your seat, take a few deep breathes, and close your eyes. Now you're ready for the inner eye switch exercise.

~ 112 ~

# Inner Eye Switch

With your eyes shut, imagine your favorite golf course. Imagine a par four that you love to play. Then imagine the backdrop of the hole. Imagine how that backdrop sets up the perfect stage for you to play your favorite shot into.

Once the stage is set, imagine playing a magnificent tee shot into the backdrop of the hole. Imagine the ball in flight, how it will land, and imagine how your swing must feel to play the shot. Imagine how your swing is the stroke of the brush that paints the shot into the backdrop. Imagine the shot coming to its final resting place.

*Now, add 2 + 2 in your head.* What do you get? Come back to your favorite golf course now.

Imagine where your golf ball is resting in the fairway. Imagine it waiting there, fascinated by the possibility of flying through the air one more time. Imagine what your approach to the green looks like. Imagine where you want the ball to land. Imagine how it is going to land. Is it going to land softly, is it going to spin, is it going to release? Imagine how that landing will feel. Imagine how the ball will fly to the green. Imagine the flight's trajectory. Imagine how your swing will feel.

*Now, multiply 10 times 12 in your head.* What do you get? Come back to the golf course.

Imagine how your ball lies in relation to the hole. Are you left with a uphill putt, or a downhill putt? Imagine whether it's going to break right or left. Imagine whether it's fast or slow. Imagine the exact line of the putt and imagine the ball rolling end-over-end down the line. Imagine the ball falling into the hole with perfect speed. Imagine how your stroke will feel. *Now, divide 50 by 2 in your head.* What do you get? Now bring your focus back to the golf course. Imagine picking the ball out of the hole, and how you feel. *Now, add 12 + 31 in your head.* What do you get?

As I do this exercise with students, I talk them through the exercise providing them with the story, and the mathematics to calculate. When you train on your own, you will have to direct yourself through the exercise. If you have a friend or playing companion who is willing to try this exercise, you can help each other out. Eventually you'll get the hang of doing it on your own.

As you imagined being on the golf course and playing golf, where did those images happen? As you calculated the mathematics in your head, where did they happen? Did they happen in the same place, or did they happen in different locations? If you were truly imagining your play, then your images were experienced through your inner eye. Whereas, when you were calculating it happened in your thinking mind. It may seem difficult to get the distinction the first time around, that's alright.

Continue to execute the exercise until you are aware of where your images come from as compared to your thoughts. Once you have the hang of the exercise, you can speed up the process of switching between calculations and images. For example, close your eyes and imagine a tee shot, now add 3 + 6. Then imagine an approach shot; now multiply 4 times 8. Imagine a chip shot; then divide 33 by 3. Imagine a long putt; then add 5 + 6 + 12. Imagine holing a putt; then multiply 2 times 5.

As you switch back and forth with more frequency, it will become apparent where both processes are happening. Again the goal of this exercise is to become aware of the distinction between these two processes. There is nothing to get right. You simply need to be aware of how images happen for you, how thinking happens for you, and the difference between the two.

# Mind's Eye Imagery

Another good way of developing the strength of your inner eye is by playing a round of golf in your minds eye. When I played competitively full time, I would play each course in my mind's eye the night before each tournament round. Actually, I would do it all week long. During our practice rounds, the pin positions for the tournament were often sprayed on the green a couple of days ahead of time. The marks would be color coded, so we would know which mark was for which day. During the practice round I would note each pin location in my yardage book. I would also practice putting to the marks from many different directions. As I noted each pin position, I would also note where I wanted my approach shot to end up to leave me the best chance of holing my birdie putt.

Before I went to bed each night, I would make a game plan for the following day. As I was lying in bed waiting to fall asleep, I would play the course with my inner eye. I would begin by imagining how I was going to feel on the first tee. I would imagine warming up properly so that I would feel good on the first tee. I would imagine the anticipation of my first tee shot. I was always inspired by the first shot of the round.

I loved teeing off in front of an audience, whether my audience was three people, or one hundred. The more people, the more inspired I was. I would then imagine each shot of the round. I would imagine how challenging they would be. I would imagine the pressure I would feel. I would imagine what I would do if I became distracted along the way. Each night I would imagine playing the next days round two or three times before I fell asleep.

The more I executed the exercise, the more identically I would imagine playing each round. The questions, doubts, and uncertainties that I had begun with would disappear, and I actually experienced playing the type of golf I wanted to play. When I got to the course the next day, it was as if I had already finished the round successfully. I felt at ease, as if I had played the course magnificently time and time again. That gave me tremendous confidence as I played my way throughout each round. The last tournament I played in 1992 before I got injured, I remember giving my caddy a written copy of my game plan. I had written down exactly where I wanted to play each tee shot, and each approach shot. I had written exactly how far away from the pin I wanted each approach shot to end up, and from what angle I would be putting.

I gave the copy to my caddy so that he would know my mind-set and how I was going to approach the round. He charted my round, and at the end of they day, he told me I had only missed one shot. Every other shot was played the way I had been imagining them. Of course I missed my share of putts, but that's the part of my game that gives me the most challenge. It was extremely satisfying playing those types of rounds. It was the type of golf I worked my whole life towards playing.

Shortly after that tournament, I suffered some severe injuries. I was sidelined from the game for over four years. At one point I was told I would never play golf again. I went through two operations, and much therapy. Throughout the four years of waiting I continued to imagine playing golf. I continued to teach the approach I have described in this book. Even though I was unable to physically play golf during those four years, I imagined doing so. I found out that imagining my golf was just as powerful, and just as much an experience as playing physically. The result of my inner training was that I shot 70 on the first round of golf I'd played after my long layoff. It was also the most satisfying round of golf I'd ever played because I knew I was getting a second chance in life.

Of course my struggles were far from finished. I still had a lot of therapy to maintain. My injuries were such that it would take many years to restore balance into my body. However those years have been spent well. They have taught me a lot about my inner resolve and the workings of my inner golfer. Throughout it all, I have always kept open the possibility that I would regain my physical form. And I believed that maintaining an image of a favorable future would guide me through my struggles and into that future.

In short, I have never lost that image in my mind's eye. For me it is a reality, the stronger the powers of my inner eye, the more favorable my future becomes.

# Eyes Closed Practice

### Balance for Passive Awareness
### Clubface for Active Awareness
### Where's It Going for Spacious Awareness

Another good way to become aware of how your inner eye captures your images is by playing shots with your eyes closed. Eyes closed training is a good way of getting in touch with your inner self. With your eyes closed you learn to trust your senses. You learn to maintain balance through body awareness (passive awareness), you learn to let your inner golfer direct your swing (active awareness), and you learn to pay attention to where the ball is going without having to look at it (spacious awareness).

To play good shots with your eyes closed, you need to have courage and trust. You must have the courage to play through the uncertainty you feel when your closed eyes blind you to the every day visual world. You must learn to trust your inner golfer, who has vision even when your eyes are closed. You must believe in the process of imagery.

As you play shots with your eyes closed, I want you to focus in on one purpose at a time. Although there are many things you can focus on, I'm going to suggest you use eyes closed "balance awareness" for training mindfulness of passive awareness, "clubface awareness" for training mindfulness of active awareness, and "where's it going" mindfulness for spacious awareness. I also suggest you stick with passive awareness training until you are confident in your attentiveness to eye's closed balance. Then you can move onto eye's closed clubface awareness, followed by spacious awareness of where your shots are going. Once you have trained with these for a while, you can choose some of your own.

As you begin performing your eyes closed awareness, you can do it in your house or somewhere outside with enough room to swing a club freely. At first it is unnecessary to play golf shots. You can play shots on a range at some point in the future when you are truly confident in your eyes closed awareness. Locate a place to swing, and assume your address position. Close your eyes, imagine your target, and imagine playing a shot to the target. Next, imagine the swing that will send the ball to your target. Then swing. As you swing with your eyes closed, pay attention to the quality of your balance. Notice whether your swing feels in balance or out of balance. Notice what balance point feels best: at address, during your swing, and in your finish.

When you start training with your eyes closed, you may find it difficult to trust your swing. If that is the case, then swing in slow motion. While swinging in slow motion it will be easier to pay attention to what is happening. As you become more and more comfortable swinging in slow motion with your eyes closed, you can step up the momentum of the swing. Eventually you will be able to swing at your regular speed and maintain balance.

If you have a hard time paying attention to your balance, notice whether your thoughts are getting in the way. If that is the case, utilize "awe-ing" as you swing. While "awe-ing," you will relax your body and quiet your mind, that will make it easier to notice your balance point. Once you've trained long enough, you'll be aware of how to maintain balance throughout your swing. You'll begin to trust the feel of your swing, and the fears of moving through the world without your eyes will diminish. You'll become more comfortable with the visions of your inner eye. You'll find a connexion there. Then once you feel ready, transition to active awareness training by attending to the squareness of the clubface with your eyes closed. One last note before we move onto active awareness training. If you want to deepen your passive awareness you can simply use eyes closed awareness and "awe-ing" together. Used together, they are the best vehicle for opening your passive awareness mechanism while developing your most natural swing.

To develop clubface awareness, begin training with your eyes closed and paying attention to your breath and your balance. Once settled in, start swinging in slow motion and keep your attention on the surface of the clubface. Imagine two eyes looking out of the face of the club. The goal of mindfulness of clubface awareness is to be able to know exactly where those eyes are looking throughout the whole swing. This can be a difficult task, especially if this is your first experience with active awareness training. Continue to swing in slow motion until you are truly aware of where the clubface is facing. The more aware you are of the clubface relationship throughout the whole swing, the more naturally you will square the clubface as you swing through the ball toward your target. If thoughts continue to disrupt your attentiveness to the clubface relationship, then I suggest you exercise active awareness while sitting still. If that is the case, proceed to the Focal Confidence section of this chapter. You can find sitting still mindfulness training in that section. Once you are confident in your eyes closed balance awareness and your eyes closed clubface awareness, you are ready to go out to the range and train spacious awareness.

Now that you are ready to train on the range, there will be more pressure put on the situation. Therefore, as you take your eyes-closed training to the next level, you will have to find a little more courage to get you through the uncertainty of the moment. With each shot, put your worries aside, avoid thinking about how other people will perceive you if miss or top a shot, such considerations will make you mental instead of mindful.

I often find that, when my students train with their eyes closed, they feel a need to announce it to the world that they are swinging with their eyes closed. They want people to know that if they miss it, it was because their eyes were closed. However, whether eyes closed or eyes open, it is still your responsibility to stay focused. It is also your responsibility to stay focused on the possibility of playing a magnificent shot. What other people think about is unimportant. What you are aware of, what you are focused on, and how committed you are to a favorable future is important. Let people make their comments. Let yourself miss shots. And learn to develop confidence in your inner golfer, the type of confidence that brings extraordinary experiences into your life.

Now it is time to apply your attentiveness to playing the game in the presence of the world, and that will involve spacious awareness. The process begins by being passively aware of your balance. Then you activate the swing by imagining the shot you are going to play. With trust and absorption you swing with active attentiveness. Then, as the ball flies through the air, you simply stay attentive to where it is flying.

When I was first introduced to this training, Fred Shoemaker would watch the shots for me and ask me, "Where's it going?" With all the attentiveness I could muster I gave it my best guess. In the beginning it was a guess. However, over time I began to tune into what was in the space around me. I was able to pay attention to exactly where the ball was going, and could tell him with certainty where it was going. Eventually I was able to be aware of where the shot was flying within 3 feet of where it actually flew. After that point in my training I would step up on the tee and ask myself, where is this one going? Then I'd stripe the ball at my target. If I was nervous and had trouble tuning in, then I'd take a couple of deep breaths, feel the swing, and ask myself once again, "where's it going." I'd snap right back into my focus and play the ball to my target. Then on occasion I'd still get distracted by unwanted thought visitors in the middle of my swing. However, these occurrences were so infrequent that I chalked them up to being human.

As you get ready to exercise your "Where's It Going" training, set up to each ball and imagine the shot you want to play. Imagine everything about the shot that is projected out into the playing field. Imagine what's out there. Get absorbed into the image. Try to find something that fascinates you about the shot. Capture the image, then swing. As you swing, notice whether you stay absorbed in the image of the shot, or whether something distracted your focus away from the image. Notice what type of things distract you away from the image. Notice where your attention goes when you become distracted. Notice how those distractions generally come in the form of thoughts.

I believe you can focus so strongly that so-called inherent distraction will passed you right by. For example, one

~ 122 ~

day I was playing Ko'olau Golf Course in Hawaii. Ko'olau Golf Course is rated the toughest golf course in the United States. So it has more distractions than just about any golf course I have played.

However, I made my home at Ko'olau as their Director of Instruction, and I loved playing the course. It is carved right into the jungle and it is one of the most beautiful courses I've ever played. On the particular day I'm thinking of, I was playing with a couple of friends. I happened to be playing extremely well, and one of my friends was struggling terribly. When we reached the tenth tee, I teed up my ball as normal, focused on my shot and striped the shot down the middle. After watching the ball come to rest, I turned to walk towards my golf cart. As soon as I turned, I was looking my friend right in the face. He had a strange look on his face. So I said, "What?" He turned to our other friend in the cart and said, "He never heard a thing, did he?" She said, "nope." It turns out my friend had bought an extra bag of potato chips and had proceeded to smash it up while I was swinging. He had apparently been trying to distract me throughout the whole front nine.

The fact is my focus was so strong, that I was unable to hear what was going on right behind me. That's concentrated focus. So when I see professional golfers complain about cameras snapping, I wonder, "Were they really focused in the first place?" Sure we can justify reasons why golf fans ought to be quiet, but if basketball players can stay focused amongst all the confusion they see behind the basket while shooting free throws, then golfers can focus with cameras snapping. It interests me that we are alright with birds chirping, and planes flying overhead. We are ok with cars driving by on a road next to a tee box. However, we complain about cars honking their horns, and people snapping cameras. Any sound can be distracting, so why are some sounds perceived as appropriate and others inappropriate? I believe it's because the golfer chooses it to be that way.

The reality is that it's the golfer's individual responsibility. If you learn how to focus your active awareness properly, you can be aware of how to focus so strongly that you will minimize recognition of the distractions. Of course some distractions will still work their way into your thinking mind. It is a reality of being human. When it happens, avoid making excuses, accept that it happened, and get focused on the next shot. Leave your distracted efforts in your past and focus in on the possibility that your next swing will be extremely focused.

Training with your eyes closed will help you learn to get through these deceptions. It will help you learn to have confidence in yourself and your ability to focus. It will help you learn to take responsibility for your actions. While swinging with your eyes closed, you will learn that you play well when you focus well, and you play poorly when you become mentally distracted. Since you will be aware of the distinction between inner focus and distracted thought, you can simply get back to focusing on your next swing.

As you gain confidence in your ability to stay focused on the image throughout the whole swing, start asking yourself, "where's it going?" Then take a guess. Once you've guessed, open your eyes and look for the ball. Notice how close you got to being truly aware of where the ball was going. If you need to, find a friend that will exercise "Where's It Going" with you. Play shots with your eyes closed, then tell your friend where you imagine it's going. Your friend then simply tells you where it went. Without judging your guess, play another shot and guess again. Eventually, you'll actually be seeing where the ball is going with your inner eye.

# Awe-ing Practice

**Awe-ing** is an exercise that helps quiet the mind and relax your body. With a quiet mind and a tension free body, your inner eye is open to imagine your shots freely. The main goal of awe-ing training is to learn how to swing while maintaining as constant, relaxed, and deep an awe as possible. As you swing, you say "awe" out loud. It's the same sound as "Ahhh." I choose to spell it "awe" instead of "ah," because I think you will be in *awe* of what happens with your game once you are able to "awe" consistently well.

As you exercise awe-ing, you will undoubtedly feel a lot of tension throughout your swing. At the moment you experience tension, you will feel an inflection in the awe. You will be able to both hear and feel the inflection. It will sound funny, and the golfers practicing next to you may think, "What the heck is that person doing." Just like the eyes closed drill, it is unimportant what other people think. Your job is to become aware of how well you are awe-ing, and what you need to do to swing with a perfect awe.

The process of how the awe influences your swing is quite amazing. In order to maintain the perfect awe, all the components of your body have to move in perfect synchronization with each other. That means the quality of your timing and your rhythm must be perfect. So, the better your awe, the better your timing and rhythm become. Once you understand the basic fundamentals of each shot, you can use awe-ing training to fine-tune your timing and your rhythm.

While awe-ing, your main focus is on the quality of your awe. As you prepare to awe, I want you to ask yourself this question, "How do I need to swing in order to feel an undisturbed awe?" Avoid calculating this technically. It's a feeling. Ask this question to your inner golfer, and wait for the response. You may experience the response as a gut feeling, or you may see it in your inner eye. Let the question and the inner responses guide your practice. If your inner golfer directs you to adjust your swing path, then do so. If your inner golfer directs you to adjust your set, then do so. If your inner golfer directs you to adjust your turn and your weight shift, then do so. Finally, do whatever you need to do to blend it all together to perform a long, smooth, rhythmic awe. Once you've reached this fine-tuning stage, the subtle forces of the game have greater understanding than any intellectual theory. What I mean is, despite what theory you might believe to be technically correct, if your inner golfer directs you to adjust your motion so that you can achieve a better awe. Then do it. The fact is, your inner golfer knows more about what's correct for *you*, than your intellect does. So, whenever possible listen to your inner golfer.

# Swing Sayings

Using swing sayings is a great way of integrating the intentions of the mind with the actions of the body. The key to a performance-oriented saying is that it captures the essence of what the swing is intending to accomplish. For example, in the short game I toss the ball with the golf club. Then, on the golf course I use the tossing method in my short game. Since my intention is to toss the ball to the hole I say, "toss-hole." I say "toss" during the backswing and "hole" during the follow-thru.

The neat thing about the swing saying is that I believe that tossing is the best way for me to play those short game shots, and the saying captures the intent of my performance, so my thinking mind is satisfied that the saying will carry the intellectual content of my intention throughout the performance.

You might say the saying occupies the mind with a productive belief, and as long as the thinking mind believes in the importance of the sayings content, it will attend to the saying without letting other thought visitors interrupt the process. You might say the swing saying occupies the thinking mind so it stays out of the way of active awareness.

This is much like giving a child a video to watch, or a game to play, when you need to get work done. If the child is uninterested in the game or the video, then he will continue to pull on your shirt sleeve or hang onto your leg for attention. And with the child constantly trying to get your attention you will be unable get any work done. So, you find something to distract the child with. You find something the child can stay interested in long enough for you to get your work done. And as long as the child is occupied by the video, or the game, you can perform your job efficiently. The mind is much like the inquisitive child starving for attention. If you give it something to believe in, it will stay out of your way while you attend to your performance routine.

There are many swing sayings you can use. I use "roll-hole" in putting, "toss-hole" in the short game, "one-two" in my control swings, and "1001-1002" in my full swings for rhythm and timing. Even "awe-ing" works as a good pacifier for my thinking mind.

Many of my students use "swing-back swing-thru," or "turn-back turn-thru" in their full swings. "Swing-smooth swing-smooth" is often used for rhythm. I've even had students use sayings like "super-smooth" and "jelly-donut" to remind themselves of something real smooth for good rhythm. Any saying is fine as long as it interests you and captures your attention for the duration of the swing. If you believe it helps, if you believe it is important to the task, then the saying can occupy the thinking mind effectively.

Finally, when you first use swing sayings, just saying the saying might be distracting. It will be distracting because it is distracting you from your habitual habit of thinking too much, and even that can be unfamiliar. Eventually you'll find sayings you believe in, and you'll say them without thinking.

# Best out of Ten

To develop confidence in your ability to focus, use the Best-Out-Of-Ten drill. Play ten shots one at a time. After each shot assess on a scale from one to ten (ten being the best) how well you stayed absorbed into the chosen image. Each time your focus was rated a 7 or higher you get one point. At the end of all ten shots, note how many points you've accumulated. Continue practicing until you're averaging 8 out of ten points. Eight out of ten is 80 percent, which is good performance.

If you're unsure of how good the focus was, you can use swing sayings for feedback. Say the saying out loud as you swing. Saying it out loud provides good feedback. Our society has an underlying premise, "if you say your going to do something you should do it." When you say the saying out loud and the motion feels like the saying, then the whole experience seems right. If you say it out loud and it feels different than what you were saying, then it becomes immediately obvious that the motion was something other than the intended swing. At which point you'll feel silly. You'll undoubtedly look around to see if anyone heard you saying it and saw that you failed to do it. Avoid letting your ego get too caught up in being self conscious, we all make mistakes. Simply get back to training and pay attention to the good feedback.

In the beginning you may only experience 3 or 4 out of ten good focuses. That's alright. Let that rating be your baseline. It's just a starting point. As you continue to train you'll find the self-motivation to average 5, then 6, then 7, and finally 8 out of ten. I've never met a golfer who could settle for less than 7 out of 10 good performances.

# Focal Confidence

I'm going to suggest a meditation exercise that will help develop your ability to maintain your focus for longer periods of time in an active state of awareness. For developing greater confidence in putting, I give students a drill I call the confidence drill. In this drill the goal is to make one hundred putts in a row without missing one. If you miss one you must start over.

Most students begin the drill with the ball only a foot or so away from the hole. Then as they become more and more confident, they are able to move the ball further and further away from the hole and still make one hundred putts in a row. I like to use this same method in an active awareness exercise designed to develop greater confidence in our focal abilities.

The exercise I like to use begins by sitting still in a peaceful place. Close your eyes and begin attending to your breath as you would in passive awareness practice. Once you feel settled in start counting each breath, in and out – 1, in and out –2, in and out – 3, until you can reach 10 counts without a thought interfering with your mindful practice. Once you are able to count to 10 without mental interference set the goal of counting to 20, then 30, then 40. With the ultimate goal of being able to count to 100 breaths without mental interference interrupting the process. Remember, if any random thoughts disrupt your mindfulness of breathing and counting, you must start over. When you can continually count to 10 without distractions you will have a solid focal foundation. Then as you climb the ladder, you will notice your focus getting stronger and stronger. You will also notice your confidence in your ability to focus grow stronger.

When you are confident in this exercise you can use it on the golf course when you feel a mental condition sneaking up on you. Maybe it will happen when you need to wait for the group a head of you. Maybe it will happen as you are waiting to make what you perceive as a crucial putt. Whenever you find yourself sinking into the mental chatter, take a mental time out by engaging in an awareness exercise.

This confidence drill for focus can be a good one to get you back on track with your performance routine. While your playing partners are putting out, simply close your eyes and start counting your breaths to ten without mental interference. When you open your eyes you will feel refreshed, look around and enjoy the moment. Then step into your performance routine and play the shot.

# Chapter Twelve
## *The Edge: The Gift Of Wholeness*

Awakening a new vision begins the process of building the golfer's edge. Nurturing the vision with a warrior-competitor attitude furthers the development of the edge. Being genuine personalizes the process, giving you the sense of having an edge. Being open-minded allows you to adjust and adapt when needed, that deepens your personal edge. Being truly prepared gives confidence to the edge. Having confidence in your performance routine will give you the competitor's edge. Being able to recommit, or reinvent, yourself at anytime gives you the confidence that you will stay the course under pressure, and staying the course will help you maintain the edge. Being purposeful will make the golfer's edge whole. Finally, engaging in mindful training as well as exercises for better performance will facilitate keeping the whole process in top working order.

As far as applying the golfer's edge, exercising your performance routine with absorption and trust brings all your training and preparations into a whole package, one that gives you the edge. When you truly know for yourself that you have the whole package, everything you do will have deeper conviction, and such conviction will bring alive the ongoing attitudes, beliefs, perceptions, and disposition that embodies the warrior-competitor edge.

People are always looking for that one thing that gives them the edge. But it's never just one thing in life, or one thing in golf, that gives you the edge. It's having the whole package.

The last piece that brings the whole package to the state of being whole may seem like "the thing," but it was just "the last thing" to make the package whole. Without everything else being in place first, the "last" thing is just another piece of the puzzle.

Great performers like Jerry Rice are known for their preparation and training. I assure you he has the whole package. Even if he does not talk about the vision, the attitude, the open mindedness, or any other part of the whole package, he still has the whole package.

In golf, people often like to talk about Hogan's Secret. They talk about it as if Ben Hogan had one little piece of knowledge that was the secret to the game. If he had one piece of knowledge it was that he knew he needed the whole package, and he set out to satisfy that package in much the same way as I've described "Creating The Golfer's Edge." So, if you want to leave your own modest legacy to the game, if you want to experience a type of mastery that other golfers look up too, or if you simply want to consistently play your best golf, then I suggest you get committed whole-heartedly to the process of *Focusing On Golf* in such a way that you *"Create The Golfer's Edge."*

*Focus on golf – Creating the Golfer's Edge* is just part of EA Tischler's New Horizons Golf Approach. The complete approach is organized into 4 stages. Stage One – Developing Your Fundamentals. Stage Two is about applications and techniques. Stage Three covers your biomechanics and Stage Four is about playing the game.

The approach is organized to help golfers of all skill levels achieve their goals. Whether beginner, avid golfer or professional you are certain to find the answers you are looking for within the New Horizons Golf Approach.

# NEW HORIZONS GOLF

*A JOURNEY INTO THE EXPERIENCE*

Inquire about New Horizons Golf Schools that cover Mastering Putting, Fore54 Stroke Saving Skills, The Fundamentals, Impact Dynamics, Power Stacking and Power-of-3 Golf Biomechanics. Visit www.newhorizonsgolf.com to find out where you can attend one of our schools.

EA Tischler is the Founder and Director of Instruction of the New Horizons Golf Approach. He grew up in California's San Francisco Bay Area. EA attended U.C. San Diego where he was the golf team captain. In 1989 he turned professional, and has been playing and coaching ever since. In 1991 he began playing on the Golden State Tour. During that period he honed his game to a +4.5 handicap. Then in 1992 he was injured and was unable to play for four years. In 1994 he moved to Hawaii where he became known as the "Pro's-Pro." As a player he has compiled 8 hole-in-ones, 2 double eagles, and set 15 course records. As a coach he has helped dozens of golfer achieve their dreams of being touring professional, has self-published 18 golf instructional book, has invented and patented a variety of training aids, and in 2000 EA was voted as one of Hawaii's top teachers in the August issue of Golf Digest Magazine. Feel free to email EA at newhorizonsgolfer@yahoo.com.